SPIRITUAL WARRIOR

Making the Mind Your Best Friend

B.T. SWAMI

HARI NAMA PRESS

Copyright © 2003 by John E. Favors

All rights reserved. No part of this book may be reproduced, stored in a retrieval system, or transmitted in any form, by any means, including mechanical, electronic, photocopying, recording, or otherwise, without prior written consent of the publisher.

Hari-Nama Press gratefully acknowledges the BBT for the use of verses and purports from Srila Prabhupada's books. All such verses and purports are © Bhaktivedanta Book Trust International, Inc.

The publisher gratefully acknowledges the kind permission of Goloka Books in allowing us the use of their artwork for incorporation into our cover design.

First printing 2004
Second edition printing: Amazon KDP 2020 version 1.1

Cover and interior design by Subala dasa / Ecstatic Creations
Cover artwork by Philip Malpass / Goloka Books

ISBN 9798640208405

Spiritual Warrior

Conquering the Enemies of the Mind

Dedication

I dedicate this book to my Aunt Rose, who shared with me her *mantra*: "I am blessed by the best, and will not settle for anything less."

Contents

Acknowledgements 1
Foreword 3
Editor's Preface 7
Author's Preface 11
Introduction 13
Chapter 1: Internal Dialogue 17
  Beyond the Externals • The Influence of Karma • Accessing Our Authentic Self • Initiating Change • Identify the Source • Obstacles on the Path of Devotion • A Cry for Help • Changing Our Internal Associations • Find the Source • Questions and Answers

Chapter 2: The Importance of Short-Term Goals . . 45
  A Gradual Progression towards the Goal • Practice Makes Perfect • A Ship without a Rudder • A Means to Reach the End • Evaluate the Goal • Find a Project • Rules and Regulations Necessary but Secondary •

Small Achievements Increase Enthusiasm • Resolute Determination • The Guru and the Disciple • Questions and Answers

Chapter 3: An Attitude of Gratitude 75

Everything Rests Upon the Lord • What Blocks the Development of Gratitude • The Enemies of the Mind • Lack of Thankfulness • Excessive False Ego • What Supports Gratitude • Selflessness • Recognizing the Meaning in Life • Remove Yourself from the Center • The Importance of Forgiveness • Seeing the Extraordinary in the Ordinary • Attitude is Crucial • Blessed by the Best • A Lesson in Every Situation • Hearing from the Scriptures • Access Gratitude in Your Own Lives • Questions and Answers

Chapter 4: The Necessity of Enthusiasm 111

Enthusiasm Leads to Success • Misdirected Enthusiasm • Find Time for Introspection • Essence of Spiritual Life • The Dangers of Apathy • Causes of Stagnation • Six Activities Spoil Devotional Service • What Hinders Enthusiasm • Six Principles Guarantee Enthusiasm • Symptoms of Success • Pastimes from the Scriptures • The Perfect Offering • The Love of a Devotee • Beyond Limitations • Enthusiastic Ecstasy • Run Enthusiastically Towards the Door • Questions and Answers

Chapter 5: The Need for Constant Mindfulness . . . 149

Recognize the Essence • The Opulences of God • Well Done, My Darling, Well Done • Find the Miracles through Mindfulness • Questions and Answers

Chapter 6: The Perfect Escape 187

Escape from the Abode of Misery • Anxiety Versus Excitement • Introspect • A Mission and A Vision • Find a Permanent Solution to the Misery • Follow a Genuine Plan of Escape • Our Consciousness Creates Our Escape • The Need for Guidance • On the Verge of Escape • Questions and Answers

Chapter 7: Going Deeper by Pretending **217**
    Devotional Service Requires Spiritual Acceleration •
    Pretend • Act According to Reality • We Have the Power
    to Make a Difference • Effort Versus Mercy • Desire
    and Deserve • Limitations of Materialistic Activities •
    Healthy Pretending is the Authentic Activity • Sincerity
    is Essential • Unless We Advance, We Will Fall Down •
    Questions and Answers

Epilogue **253**
Notes **255**
Glossary **257**
Bibliography **263**
Index **267**
About the Author **273**

x   Spiritual Warrior V

Acknowledgements

I would sincerely like to thank Lauren Kossis for the initial editing of the book. I would also like to thank Jambavan Dasa for Sanskrit editing and Jason Gerick and Lisa Webb for proofreading. I would like to thank all of my disciples who transcribed the many audiotapes, and Adam Kenney, Krista Helfer, and Stewart Cannon for the layout, final editing, and all things necessary to bring this book to press. I would also like to thank the following people from the United Kingdom for financing the printing of *Spiritual Warrior IV* and *V*—Kamlesh Gandhi, Jean Williams, Eddie Anobah, and Citi-sakti Dasi. You are wonderful spiritual warriors who are eager to assist others in conquering the enemies of the mind in order to make the mind the best friend.

2   Spiritual Warrior V

Foreword

His Holiness Bhakti Tirtha Swami inspires us to be spiritual warriors in life, following the tradition of Arjuna, the Great Warrior depicted in the *Bhagavad-gita*. However, in this book he achieves this by updating the metaphors and language in a way that will reach out to many people in today's world. It is a message of love, faith and devotion that constantly inspires.

At first, the mind is likened to a field that needs plowing and harrowing before the seeds of spiritual growth can be sown. Effort is needed to clear the mind of negative thinking, beliefs and destructive self-imagery. The subject of addictions is treated in a fashion similar to the 12-step recovery program. Being humble enough to surrender to a higher power and realizing that one can only recover one step at a time are two helpful walking sticks for the struggling addict. It is the spiritual intoxication, the natural ecstasy of the soul that the addict was seeking. However, the battle of life requires the development of much mastery. By mastering our minds and channeling our desires through short-term goals that we personally value, a gradual spiritual confidence emerges. Once again, what motivates us in this struggle is the love of God.

The Swami also addresses one of the great issues of our time: the forces of materialism, which have captured the desires of the great majority of people on our planet. However, he correctly points out that this affects our attitudes and expectations. Material success can lead to greed and material failure results sometimes in poor self-esteem. Both create a false attitude, which prevents us from seeing the opportunities in life and the richness within us. Life's problems may affect us, but instead of being negative, we can try to see a valuable lesson in every situation. Even when we are stuck, and we don't realize it, the situation of stuckness begins to teach us something. By overcoming this in ourselves, we overcome the problems of suffering and duality.

I found that the most valuable contribution of this text came from the beautiful meditations on mindfulness in breathing, walking, talking, hearing, eating, seeing, reading and sleeping. These meditation practices are both beautiful, inspiring and practical at the same time in helping the devotee to transform their negative mind scripts and to transmute the negative emotions. The spiritual practices of invoking the presence of Krishna in our everyday interactions and of "helpful pretending" i.e. acting as though you are already a spiritual warrior, are powerful—"right actions help one to develop right consciousness."

In the last chapter, the Swami expounds on the doctrine of *karma* in an enlightening manner that is appropriate to our time. He explains how our minds interact with the Universal forces and shows how we can create good *karma* and how we can transform bad *karma* into something really positive. He also warns us that on the spiritual path we go up or down, but we cannot rest on our laurels or we will begin to slip downwards.

I found this book growing on me as I proceeded, realizing the vital importance of faith, devotion and surrender on the spiritual path, and that if we are to follow such a path successfully as part of our everyday life, we really need to develop the qualities of the spiritual warrior.

—Nigel Hamilton MA (Couns. Psych),
Dipl. ClinPsych & Social Psych, Director of
The Centre for Counselling & Psychotherapy
Education, London, UK

Editor's Preface

The Spiritual Warrior series consists of lectures given by His Holiness Bhakti Tirtha Swami (Swami Krishnapada) to a wide variety of live radio and television audiences around the world, over a period of several years. Since the topics were originally presented in spoken form, the style is conversational and informal. In the editing process, we have modified the text to enhance readability, yet sought to preserve some of the verbal nuances that would maintain the mood of the original presentations. In this way, we hope to create an atmosphere that literally makes you part of the audience so that you can experience the powerful presence of the speaker as he shares essential nourishment for the soul.

We would like to mention several other stylistic considerations. In the course of his discussions, Bhakti Tirtha Swami includes perspectives from many different spiritual philosophies; however, because his audiences are composed mainly of people in the Christian and Vedic traditions, he makes the most extensive references to these scriptures. At times, he uses Sanskrit terminology from the Vedas, a vast body of ancient scriptures originating from the area of the world known today as India. We have endeavored to keep many of these terms and have tried to explain them within the context of the discussion. When coming upon such terms, if you need additional information and clarification, we invite you to consult the glossary. However, there are some terms we would like to initially clarify:

- When His Holiness B.T. Swami refers to the one God that we all know of, he uses different terminologies. Sometimes he says the Supreme Lord, the Supreme Personality of Godhead, Mother-Father God, or Krishna.

- He often uses the word "devotees." He is drawing attention to those spiritualists who are connected to the Vedic tradition as well as to all aspiring spiritualists who are embarking on the spiritual journey.

- He also uses the term "nine-fold process," which refers to various activities that a person engages in during his or her spiritual practices of devotion to God, such as hearing about the Lord, speaking about Him, remembering Him, praying to Him, serving Him, fully surrendering, and so on.

Furthermore, the end of each chapter includes many of the questions and answers exchanged during the original lectures. We hope that these will respond to some of the concerns that may arise in the course of your reading. These discussions between Bhakti Tirtha Swami and the audience may also give you different angles from which to view the topics presented. This book is the fifth volume in our Spiritual Warrior series. The first four volumes, *Spiritual Warrior I: Uncovering Spiritual Truths in Psychic Phenomena*, *Spiritual Warrior II: Transforming Lust into Love*, *Spiritual Warrior III: Solace for the Heart in Difficult Times*, and *Spiritual Warrior IV: Conquering the Enemies of the Mind*, are already in print and have been translated into several different languages, along with His Holiness' other works. The information presented in these pages is extremely rare, and we hope you will make the most of the knowledge they contain. If you take these teachings seriously, they can transform your life into a most sublime, loving adventure.

10 Spiritual Warrior V

Author's Preface

Spiritual Warrior IV: Conquering the Enemies of the Mind and *Spiritual Warrior V: Making the Mind Your Best Friend* were written at the same time. They are distinct books that stand on their own, but if read together, they compliment each other even more than the previous books in the series. About fifty-five percent of my ministry is in connection with my own Vaisnava (those who worship a personal God and are connected with what many refer to as the Hindu faith) communities and institutions around the world. The other forty-five percent of my work and teaching is in connection with the international business, medical, and interfaith communities. My special area of interest involves helping leaders in all of these communities to be more authentic, and helping spiritualists of all faith communities to rise above stagnations and blocks in order to more truly help themselves and their communities.

After recently finishing a forty-country world teaching tour in which I addressed many of the issues in *Spiritual Warrior IV* and *Spiritual Warrior V*, I wanted to make some of this material available in simple written form to provide people more facility in overcoming their *anarthas*, obstacles, blocks, and stagnations. I saw that, in all of these communities, people were getting stuck and were often experiencing intense mental suffering. As I have been praying to be more of a "global change agent" in assisting people with their suffering, *Spiritual Warrior IV* and *V* are offered in this spirit.

In Sanskrit, we call the main enemies of the mind *bhaya* (fear), *kama* (lust), *krodha* (anger), *lobha* (greed), *matsarya* (envy), *mada* (madness), and *moha* (illusion). Some of their affiliates are grief, depression, chronic anxiety, panic attacks, obsessive compulsive behavior, posttraumatic stress, and phobias to name a few. In *Spiritual Warrior IV* and *V*, I address and expose these enemies, and show ways to overcome their influences. Their existence is engendered by the false ego, which means that transforming the false ego into pure ego is the ultimate solution. *Spiritual Warrior IV* and *V* will offer the reader different spiritual technologies to accomplish this. So, once again, spiritual warriors, here is more spiritual ammunition for you in the war of waging peace and love.

Introduction

In most countries and communities, mental health has been neglected for various reasons such as a poor understanding of mental health and illness, the stigma of mental illness, and a lack of awareness of the impact poor mental health has on the individual and community. According to the World Health Organization, "depression is projected to become the leading cause of disability and the second leading contributor to the global burden of disease by the year 2020." These figures do not include the number of people who are and will be suffering from low mood, which is too mild to be classified as depression and yet severe enough to have a significant impact on their life. All too often, the society we live in has taught us to deal with the afflictions of the mind with a 'band-aid' approach wherein we try to make improvements even if only temporarily. But like any other conflict or crisis, a conflict with our own mind is a great opportunity for personal growth.

In the spectrum of awareness, we are least conscious during sleep and become progressively more conscious through waking. We progress further as we develop an awareness of the subtle realms and even more so as we reach the highest platform of consciousness—the experience and knowledge of the spiritual world and our relationship with God and the universe. Our mind is our constant companion as we advance, or regress, through this continuum. It can either function as the key that opens the door to the next level or the bolt that locks the door. Many have used and will continue to use artificial means such as drugs to achieve altered states of awareness, but these can only bring about a temporary change along with the many uncomfortable side effects.

Throughout all of our waking hours and even while we sleep, providence presents us with innumerable opportunities to transform and access our divine, pure nature. For the majority of us, our mind and senses are constantly distracting us from doing so. It is through strengthening our intelligence with spiritual knowledge and allowing our senses to experience and engage in spiritual practices that we can transform the mind. It will then act as our friend by allowing us to see every encounter and experience as a chance to break out of all our physical, psychological, and subtle boundaries and truly be ourselves. Unfortunately, the mind and the problems generated by it can overwhelm and consume us to such an extent that we can end up in a situation where our ability to think rationally is greatly diminished as in cases of severe depression, anxiety, psychosis, and drug and alcohol addictions. Only a part of our success in combating mental health problems lies in finding a cure—the majority lies in prevention.

We are already aware of the contribution that our upbringing, relationships, social circumstances, physical health, and genetics make towards the development of mental health problems, but, what role does the development and manifestation of these illnesses have in our spiritual lives and how can we use spiritual knowledge to prevent and resolve these issues? Bhakti Tirtha Swami eloquently explains the answers to both these questions not only in his previous book, *Spiritual Warrior IV: Conquering the Enemies of the Mind*, but also in this book aptly titled, *Spiritual Warrior V: Making the Mind Your Best Friend*. Bhakti Tirtha Swami has given us a wonderful set of tools to be able to turn the afflictions of the mind into a key rather than a bolt so that we can become happier and more fulfilled as each day of our life goes by. Once again, he has been kind enough to share with us his expertise in applying spiritual solutions to material problems.

If we can imbibe and practice even a few of the principles outlined in this book and use them synergistically with the biological and psychological knowledge we have, it will enable us to not only transform our lives, but we will also be able to serve others better by empowering them to transform their own lives as well. After all, we cannot give to others what we haven't got ourselves. As you turn to the next page, I pray that you will keep an open heart and mind, knowing that what you are about to read will change your life.

—Dr. Chetna Kang MBBS
SHO in Psychiatry, United Kingdom

Chapter 1

Internal Dialogue

*tenasya tadrsam rajal
lingino deha-sambhavam
sraddhatsvananubhuto 'rtho
na manah sprastum arhati*

Therefore, my dear King, the living entity, who has a subtle mental covering, develops all kinds of thoughts and images because of his previous body. Take this from me as certain. There is no possibility of concocting anything mentally without having perceived it in the previous body.
Srimad-Bhagavatam 4.29.65

Beyond the Externals

We all have an ongoing internal dialogue, or internal conversations, that develop from the aggregate of our life experiences and that we constantly repeat to ourselves. The many people in our lives often give us specific labels, which we then embrace and even directly place on ourselves. Consequently, we maintain these constant conversations within us that dictate the way we respond and behave at all times. This internal dialogue is very significant because our external behavior is only a small aspect of our real selves. For instance, during most conversations, we receive only seven percent of the message from the content itself. We receive thirty-eight percent of the message from voice, pitch, tone, and sounds, and fifty-five percent from non-verbal communication such as facial gestures and body movements.[1]

The internal dialogues of the speaker as well as the receiver affect all areas of communication. Nevertheless, most people are only aware of the externals, which obviously makes communication and our relationships in general very difficult. Most importantly, by identifying too much as physical beings, we overlook the deeper aspects of our real identity.

The Influence of Karma

Modern sociology and psychology both acknowledge that we are basically products of heredity and socialization and that we are greatly affected by our parent's genes. However, most people do not understand as clearly that although these influences do in fact affect a person, they stem from *karma* in previous lifetimes. We had certain experiences in this life, which directly affect our current thought process and the way in which we codify various aspects of our lives. However, our gender, race, language, and family, which have determined our current thought process, developed from experiences and relationships in past lives. This chain goes on and on.

We can understand the effect of *karma* by analyzing different causes and effects in just one lifetime. For instance, at the present moment, certain college students might be studying law, but their previous education in elementary and high school has enabled them to reach college and has played an important role in the development of their current intellect and understanding. The students' past knowledge also affects the way in which they use or develop their present knowledge. Furthermore, many factors played a role in the past. They spent many days in school and extensive time associating with peers, teachers, and their parents. All of these influences help create a person's mentality and will determine how he or she will continue to develop in the future. In terms of this example, it will determine the type of lawyer that each individual will become.

Similarly, our current physical, psychological, and spiritual make-up develops from our previous experiences and associations. For instance, the quality of our *sadhu-sanga* or the quality of our association with saints and devotees will have a tremendous effect on our spiritual strength and the quality of our devotion. Many wonderful factors determine the quality of devotional service and many inauspicious influences also affect our current involvement in devotional life.

Accessing Our Authentic Self

Considering these factors, if we examine any given time

period in our lives, we will remember many significant events and people who strongly affected our lives. If we combine all of these influences, we will discover the person we have now become. This is important for us because, as spiritualists, we are constantly trying to access our authentic self. We want to realize our eternal nature and understand that we actually have an eternal personality. The personality who we now identify as our self is not our real self. That personality is just a part of the external and subtle processing that goes on. Our previous lifetimes have led to this body, and both our past and current lives have led us to think, react, and respond in certain ways.

We can compare our situation to a drama. Pretend that you are an actor in a one-man play and you constantly have to change your outfit and speak differently. After awhile, the audience may no longer know your real identity, and as the actor, you may even lose sight of your true self. You might soon forget which outfit to wear or what language you originally spoke. This same confusion happens to us in the material world. We have changed our bodies and our environments so many times, and in order to survive in this hostile environment, we have dressed in so many different ways. Many of those costumes and acts have now become a part of us.

Initiating Change

We want to address this issue because it is almost impossible to rise above such blocks unless we have enough honesty to identify the source and the problem in greater depth. Many people in secular as well as in spiritual communities have so many problems and issues, which stem from their current identity and their connection to these past negative influences of socialization and internal conversations. This topic interests me because I want to help more people change, enjoy spiritual life more, have greater realizations, and have healthier associations. However, I am also addressing this issue because, in the course of my own services that involve many variegated international projects, I receive a letter almost every day from someone in a state of crisis due to these psychological factors.

As we study people, we see that they sometimes have unhealthy disturbances in their spiritual lives as a result of accepting unhealthy labels from the past. For example, some people have a problem with authority, which might stem from childhood issues. In some cases, people have had alcoholic parents or might have suffered from sexual or physical abuse, which will continue to follow them until they sufficiently address the past and forgive. They need to own the past in certain ways so that they do not continue to carry it with them or allow the dialogue to continuously force them to act in unhealthy ways at the present time. Some spiritualists cannot really embrace Krishna or God consciousness sufficiently due to a problem with authority that could also manifest in many other relationships. The problems will result from this block that they have been carrying year after year, and in some cases, it even stems from a heavy trauma in a previous lifetime.

We also need to discuss these topics for the protection of the children because we want to encourage them sufficiently. For instance, distinct correlations exist between achievement in school and self-concept. Researchers surveyed a group of young children in grade school in order to understand the role that the environment plays on their development. The children, who all came from similar backgrounds and had similar IQs, were split into two groups. The teachers told one group of children that they were high achievers, and they told the other group that they were normal but might have problems with their work. Of course, the group of children who received the extra encouragement achieved higher. Not only did they achieve higher during the evaluation, but after several years, those children also maintained that mentality. They performed more expertly in whatever they pursued. Those children who somehow felt that they could not achieve or could not rise to the challenge continued to have failures in their lives. This study shows us that we will often accept what the environment tells us and then act accordingly.

Identify the Source

A significant aspect of spiritual life involves shedding many of the patterns that we have embraced as our identity, and we begin to shed them by first identifying the source. You may want to try an exercise to help you examine your past with more precision:

- Reflect on the three most significant people in your life who have left specific impressions on your consciousness.

- Reflect on the three most important choices you have made.

- Reflect on the three most significant events in your past.[2]

When you think of these categories, remember that some of them may not have been auspicious. Some outstanding events in your life as well as past associations may have been very negative and have left deep impressions on your consciousness.

Your association with certain people may have led to the development of some of your current bad habits and the acceptance of many of those negative labels. Some of those associations have caused you to develop the internal dialogue that you hear in your mind, which distracts you from your spiritual life. As you recognize the negative influences, it is important for you to separate your self from the influence. On the other hand, if the influences were positive, you can feel grateful for any benefits you have received.

Now, please put this book aside for a few hours or a day as you write down or reflect on these three categories. After you have thought deeply about them, proceed with your reading of this chapter.

Obstacles on the Path of Devotion

As we engage our senses and minds in spiritual practices, cleansing takes place. However, any medication works along with the immune system and metabolism, which means that we must take it at the right time and in the right way. For this reason, we always have offenses to avoid so that we can get the full benefit of the potent process. It will not penetrate if there are blocks. Someone can come into the temple and see the Deities, but if they simply view the Deity as an idol, they will not benefit sufficiently from the *darsana*. Viewing the Deity in Vedic culture is not idol worship but a spiritual science meant to increase our personal association and appreciation of the Supreme Lord. However, the person who sees the Deity as an idol will have an offensive internal dialogue. Not only will they disregard the Deity, but they will also fail to sufficiently appreciate *prasadam*, or sanctified vegetarian food, because their dialogue tells them that they do not eat that type of food. Another example involves people with low self-esteem who will not be able to receive love because they feel unworthy. They basically see themselves as bad or insensitive; therefore, they do not feel that others can genuinely care for them. Unfortunately, many people will continue to think in these ways and will carry negative mindsets into their adulthood and family. They will even transmit the same negativity onto their children.

We often think that we just have to chant and pray in order to reach the goal. Yes, one should chant and follow the nine-fold process of devotional service, which includes *sravanam* (hearing), *kirtanam* (chanting), *smaranam* (remembering the Lord), *pada-sevanam* (serving the lotus feet of the Lord), *arcanam* (offering the Lord respectful worship), *vandanam* (offering prayers to the Lord), *dasyam* (becoming His servant), *sakhyam* (considering the Lord as one's best friend), and *atma-nivedam* (surrendering everything to Him). In previous ages, a devotee could practice just one of the nine-fold activities and attain perfection; however, in Kali-yuga or the Age of Quarrel and Hypocrisy, we should follow all of them since we do not execute any one of them with sufficient quality.

We also understand that other factors influence our devotional service. For instance, if we have a problem with our physical body or subtle body, it might disturb our consciousness and our spiritual life. When we feel good physically, we will often find that we have more enthusiasm to carry out our spiritual activities. Similarly, when our phobias or minds do not interfere as much, we will also have fewer obstacles and the spiritual message can penetrate more easily. In terms of the physical body, if you have some pain in your body while trying to listen to a lecture, that pain will interfere with your receptivity of the message. A phobia will also cause a disturbance. For example, if you try to listen attentively to a lecture while concerned about the safety of your child as he plays outside, the noises outside will repeatedly distract you. In another case, if you come to a lecture immediately after having an argument with your spouse, you will not fully bring yourself into the spiritual activity.

After an entire lifetime of experiences, imagine the amount of distractions that hinder our ability to internally connect with God and fully absorb our consciousness in Him. We want to have a strong internal dialogue that always thinks of the Lord and worships Him.

*man-mana bhava mad-bhakto
mad-yaji mam namaskuru
mam evaisyasi yuktvaivam
atmanam mat-parayanah*

Engage your mind always in thinking of Me, become My devotee, offer obeisances to Me and worship Me. Being completely absorbed in Me, surely you will come to Me.
Bhagavad-gita 9.34

We want to always absorb ourselves with rapt attention on the Supreme Lord and recognize Him as our greatest friend and protector. He is the ultimate goal of all our endeavors. We understand that we want to reach a certain destination, but while endeavoring to achieve that goal, we have numerous obstacles. All of these deterrents are soliciting our attention and carrying our minds away from the proper path.

We have a chance to hear wonderful instructions from the scriptures, and we have a chance to embrace them and fully enter into them. However, we are drawn away by these hindrances, and instead of dealing with them, we tend to ignore them and think that they will go away. In many cases, we find that after ten, fifteen, or even thirty years of chanting, meditating, praying, and participating in spiritual processes, these hindrances still remain. They will go away if we allow the chanting and the meditating to enter deeply into our consciousness, but if we have too many blocks, the process will not sufficiently enter and take over our existence.

Once again, please take the time to stop and reflect on the following exercise, which involves the recognition of your internal dialogue. Some studies indicate that most people maintain an internal dialogue that is over eighty percent negative. For an entire day, just notice the types of internal conversations going on within your mind. Most of us are constantly putting ourselves as well as others down in different ways. We repeatedly tell ourselves that we will fail or have no worth, along with many other negative put-downs. Also, notice in our conversations with particular people how our internal dialogue sometimes distinctly differs from what we speak out loud. Unfortunately, most of the time, the internal dialogue is negative and that which we continue to internally speak turns into our *mantra*. **Consequently, we will have more experiences related to our internal dialogue even if we externally seem to not want them.**

A Cry for Help

Recently, I received a letter from a devotee that addresses

these exact issues. It shows the effect of this internal dialogue, which stagnates and hinders the progress of spiritualists all around the world. Within this letter, we will see some different types of blockages. The devotee is trying to be very serious in her devotional life but somehow the connections are not fully taking place. She writes:

> Thank you for your kindness. I want to ask you about some problems which I have. I suffer from low self-confidence. In your book, Spiritual Warrior III, you write that a healthy family environment will affect every aspect of our lives. In my family, we never showed any feelings. My parents, especially my father, always spoke negatively to me, telling me that I was not good enough. I had read some psychology books previously, which were very helpful to me because I had a big problem with depression. Now I understand that my parents could not do much better than what they did because they didn't know any better.

She acknowledges her problem and even did some initial investigation by researching psychology books. From her research, she could understand that her parents tried, and although they did not actively try to victimize her, she was a victim since she did not receive the proper love, affection, care, and communication. At least she can understand that they also had problems within themselves.

> I am writing all of this because I still have problems with this issue and I don't know how to help myself. I made some improvements but I need some help. I am afraid that I may also not have a healthy family.

She fears that she may transmit some of these unhealthy patterns from her childhood onto her family when she marries which is very probable unless it is properly dealt with in advance.

> I also have a fear of responsibility because I feel that I may not be able to come up to a certain level. I see many bad examples. One of the reasons I came to India is to find myself in a more spiritual environment. I am hoping that maybe I can accept this way of life and this culture. I see that the people here are very seriously executing their services and duties. The society of Krishna's devotees is saving me and helping me to increase my faith, but I cannot get deeper feelings.

Although her research has helped her release some of her anxiety and anger towards her parents, she still says that she has not been able to sufficiently move through this block. In an attempt to help herself, she has changed her environment and traveled to India to be in a more simplistic environment and in a community that she hopes can help her move through that bond. It is ultimately a hope to change her internal dialogue.

The environment might be able to help her think more directly about God and lose her sense of low self-esteem. She then shares a few last points.

> I cannot get deeper feelings. I notice this when I go to the temple and participate in programs with the devotees. I am doing all the external practices but only out of duty. Consequently, I am not feeling sufficiently which leaves me very unhappy. I cannot seem to develop deeper feelings for my friends, for my parents, and for the merciful Lord.

Due to the labels that her parents have given her, she has been trained not to feel. She feels that she is a failure and insignificant. She says that this block is interfering will her ability to develop deeper relationships with her peers and friends, and to really open her heart to Krishna. What she does not say is that it also interferes with her feelings toward her spiritual master.

> I do not know how to give and accept love with my heart. I am sure that my parents love me but they never showed me their affection. Now I have my own problems expressing my feelings. I try to forgive my parents and I have a good relationship with them now externally. However, I am blaming myself and sometimes think that maybe I really was not good enough for them. And I think that this also affects my

relationships with other people. How can I find faith and respect myself? How do I find deeper compassion and love for others?

Although she knows that she carries this unhealthy internal dialogue, she cannot fully free herself. It manifests when she executes her devotional activities very mechanically. She comes to the temple and engages in her *sadhana* or spiritual practices, but she does not really give her heart or mind to the process. She also has blocks and barriers when she associates with devotees. Actually, she is fortunate in many ways because she is able to recognize the source of some of these issues and look at the past.

In my response, I told her, "Yes, your thoughts and feelings are real. They are not superficial and they need to be addressed. You definitely need help." I also stated that she has basically dealt with 75% of the problem through her ability to analyze it with honesty. However, the last 25% is the most difficult part, which I agreed to help her with. I also shared some of the other points on the internal dialogue that we have already addressed in this chapter.

In my initial response to her, I also suggested that she look closer at forgiving her parents because some signs indicate that she has not entirely forgiven them. She has given so much of her power over to them because, as she ends the letter, she still emphasizes that she does not feel good enough for them. This means that she still accepts the labels and has kept that internal dialogue playing over and over. In order to bring more closure to the situation, she needs to look closer and find a deeper way to release their labels. It also deals with forgiveness, which a person especially needs to do for themselves. It does not mean that we sanction their past behavior or consider that they parented in the proper way. Forgiveness also does not mean that she accepts those labels by considering herself a bad person. No, it means that she lets go so that she can now learn from the past and look towards the future.

Changing Our Internal Associations

This dialogue is very powerful because we are with ourselves all of the time. We are with other people sometimes but we are with ourselves every moment of the day. Imagine associating with a person who at every single moment continuously calls you a failure, a moron, an imbecile, or a problem. This person sends you constant messages that your very existence causes them pain. If someone talks to us in this way occasionally, we might later find ways to avoid them, but we must associate with our minds all of the time! The most unfortunate aspect is that we must associate with our minds even at times when we stop monitoring its thoughts.

This internal conversation is so important because we will become that which we constantly tell ourselves. The sweet part of the devotional process is that as we read the scriptures, hear the lectures, and hear the holy name, we will gradually connect our internal dialogue more and more with transcendence. After awhile, if those connections remain our healthy diet, they will transform our subtle as well as our physical body due to that level of communication. When we do not have a spiritual dialogue, we may hear, read, interact, engage in some type of *puja*, or worship for many decades, but we will still hear the same old tape in our minds. We will not completely benefit if the internal meditation completely differs from these external devotional activities.

For this reason, some very successful people in the material world have low self-esteem. Even though they have achieved so many of their goals, they still cling onto these past tapes that will play again and again. Even in this case, the girl has come into a devotional community, read the scriptures, heard many lectures, and has even researched the problem on her own but all of these positive activities have only helped her to a certain extent. Until her internal dialogue changes, she will not make a significant transition. She can repeatedly hear that we are not our bodies, Krishna is our ultimate protector and He is ready to receive us, but if her mind continues to preach the same old negative messages, she will only partially accept the spiritual truths.

As devotees, we have brought so much with us from the past and our *karma* may have unfolded as a rough past. However, by the Lord's mercy the rough past led us to embrace spiritual life because we did not want to accept orthodoxy. Many people come to spiritual life out of distress, a desire for wealth, or a desire for knowledge.

catur-vidha bhajante mam
janah sukrtino 'rjuna
arto jijnasur artharthi
jnani ca bharatarsabha

O best among the Bharatas, four kinds of pious men begin to render devotional service unto Me – the distressed, the desirer of wealth, the inquisitive, and he who is searching for knowledge of the Absolute.
Bhagavad-gita 7.16

Each category contains victims of socializations, and external and internal labeling.

We can basically summarize all of these points by saying that we will begin to seriously change when we change what we constantly tell ourselves. We associate with ourselves for the maximum amount of time, which means that we must change the nature of that association. Especially during our vulnerable times, which happen when we lack good association or feel fearful, depressed, and anxious, the mind will become even stronger. The influence of our own mind is extremely pervasive.

For example, people who have been sexually abused may tend to see it as their fault. By accepting the blame and suffering in their own life as a result, they turn to alcohol or drugs and fall into an addiction. However, by trying to erase the past through intoxications, they only compound the problem even more. Now, in order to change, the person must deal with both the addiction and the trauma simultaneously. Although they hear that drugs will destroy the body and enslave them, they continue with the habit because they cannot sufficiently change their consciousness or internal dialogue. As transcendentalists, we have great understanding about the powers and dangers of the mind. We also understand the influence of previous lives, which produces our current life. We want to eliminate those issues from our past and present lives so that we can free ourselves of those particular shackles. Then we can address the issue.

Find the Source

I would like to share one last example that also deals with

trauma. Many of these examples come from women because women often communicate more than men. As men, we have an even worse position because we hold these pains and are afraid to talk about them. This final example deals with a woman who is 100 pounds overweight and diets continuously. In some cases, she goes through successful diets but simply returns to her previous eating habits after awhile. Sometimes this scenario might result from her internal dialogue, and in other cases, she might feel needy and then substitute food for a lack of healthy relationships.

If we look deeper, this woman might have undergone a trauma in her childhood such as sexual abuse. When she begins to lose weight as an adult, she begins to attract men, and this makes her feel sexually vulnerable. These situations stimulate her consciousness and remind her of the abusive experience from her past which she never addressed sufficiently. Then she begins to overeat again because she wants to protect herself with her body image and not place herself in the same abusive situation again. A person can go on one diet after another without ever recognizing the real issue. The internal dialogue will simply remain the same, and due to fear, they put themselves in a situation that hinders their ability to transcend a particular block by this inability to identify the block.

These examples can help us reflect on the various blocks in our consciousness which return again and again and continue to haunt us. Consequently, we will simply remain a part of the deteriorating situation in the world in which people constantly divorce and children do not receive proper protection, even in spiritual communities. We will even end up transmitting our own problems to our children because we have not dealt with them sufficiently. Therefore, we impose our own weaknesses on them and unfortunately, in most cases, they will not be able to deal with them either because of their own developing internal dialogues. As devotees, we do not have to become psychiatrists, psychologists, or sociologists; however, we do need to better understand the power of the mind. The mind can be our greatest friend or our greatest enemy. These discussions should help us realize that our mind is basically our enemy until we can understand its dealings. Once we recognize how it functions, we can turn it into our best friend.

Questions and Answers

Question: In this context, how do we understand the verse in the Vedic literature, *harer nama harer nama harer namaiva kevalam kalau nasty eva nasty eva nasty eva gatir anyatha*: "In this age of quarrel and hypocrisy, the only means of deliverance is chanting the holy name of the Lord. There is no other way. There is no other way. There is no other way" (*Brhannaradiya Purana*). You acknowledge that those on the path of *bhakti-yoga* may need to look at their dysfunctional, emotional state. In one sense, a person might consider it easier to not deal with such problems because they bring up so much pain. They would rather just chant the holy name, read the *Bhagavad-gita*, and follow this verse. How would you respond to this point?

Answer: For instance, we understand that chanting the holy name is the *yuga-dharma* or the most effective prescribed activity for this age but that does not mean that we neglect prayer (*vandanam*), worship (*arcanam*), remembrance (*sravanam*), and the other activities in the nine-fold process. We do say that the chanting is the way to achieve success in Kali-yuga, but it means that we must keep it as foremost as we engage in all of our other activities. For instance, if our Deity service is not sheltered by the holy name, it then turns into idol worship. Similarly, we will not hear or read the scriptures deeply if we do not have a proper connection with the holy name. Chanting the holy name properly for full efficacy involves absorption in the complete science of *bhakti-yoga*, especially avoiding the offenses or obstacles.

Furthermore, Krishna clearly states:

> *tesam satata-yuktanam*
> *bhajatam priti-purvakam*
> *dadami buddhi-yogam tam*
> *yena mam upayanti te*

> To those who are constantly devoted to serving Me with love, I give the understanding by which they can come to Me.
> *Bhagavad-gita* 10.10

The Lord tells us that as we surrender, He rewards us accordingly. However, we need to look at the interferences, which prevent our full surrender and decrease our ability to accept God as a loving personality. If my internal dialogue tells me that love does not exist or that I am unworthy of receiving love, I will not be able to fully embrace these statements spoken by God Himself. I will not allow His words to fully enter into my consciousness. We understand that Krishna gives the medication but how do we accept it and take it fully? Certain obstacles can prevent us from taking advantage of the gifts that He makes available or cause us to move more slowly towards the goal.

Question: Are there any other ways of changing our perceptions? It seems that changing our faulty perceptions will help us realize that we are not alone and that the Lord actually loves us.

Answer: In terms of changing our perceptions, forgiveness plays a very important role because grudges cause a good deal of stagnation. For this reason, in my recent travels through Croatia, Malaysia, Russia, England, and so on, I often gave workshops on forgiveness. I gave examples of different *acaryas* and *sadhus* who underwent attack or abuse but elevated the other person. Sometimes the attack came from their own *karma*, but we want to understand how they used it to look closer at the situation and understand more about the other person.

Along with forgiveness, we must also develop a sense of compassion for ourselves as well as for others. For example, a father might carry an unhealthy dialogue with him due to a negative situation from his own past. However, if he wants to be more loving with his own children, it might help him to look closer at his own issues. In this way, he can try to be more available for his son or daughter. This means that we have to find ways to be more effective in the present, which will allow us to give and have more concern and love for our associates. It will help us develop forgiveness and compassion for those in our immediate environment as well as for ourselves. Someone who suffers from depression and phobias will constantly limit their ability to help and give love to those in their present. They will not be able to bring the best of themselves into any situation. If they are not careful, their actions will then transmit to the consciousness of their children and their children will begin to develop the same internal dialogues as well.

Another way to change these perceptions involves our

reaction to an issue. After we confront a problem, we must now find a healthy way to react. It some cases, it requires a very distinct action such as talking to the mother who knew about the abusive father but who did not attempt to stop the abuse. Some people may actually have to address the issue so that they can get rid of it and walk away from the past. We will not go deeper into it at this point because it also depends on specifics as well as general considerations but, in general, it requires forgiveness, compassion, and proper action.

The most important requirement is replacement. Even after evaluating the situation and practicing forgiveness, the internal dialogue will only change temporarily unless we replace that negative energy with positive, auspicious activities that will absorb the mind, body, and senses.

visaya vinivartante
niraharasya dehinah
rasa-varjam raso 'py asya
param drstva nivartate

> The embodied soul may be restricted from sense enjoyment, though the taste for sense objects remains. But, ceasing such engagements by experiencing a higher taste, he is fixed in consciousness.
> Bhagavad-gita 2.59

This positive absorption will reduce the tendency to revert to old patterns because although we may have moved away from the past patterns, the seeds of sin still remain. Once we pull out the weed, we have to go deeper to take out the root of the weed so that it will not come back. For this reason, alcoholics can remain abstinent for many years but then suddenly revert to the addiction when they feel weak or bewildered. Then they return to their comfort zone since it previously gave them some shelter, fulfillment, and stimulation. After returning to the alcohol, the same internal dialogue begins once again and the same old tape begins to play.

Most people in the world are dealing with these issues, and as Kali-yuga progresses in just these next few years, we will see this problem increase more and more on the planet. People are distinctly having more mental challenges due to the abuse of Mother Bhumi or Mother Earth because the abuse of natural resources is constantly creating more general mental pollution. As more people have mental challenges, those problems will spill over into the environment and in turn affect many more people. Even if we somehow do not have any of these issues in our lives, we must still be careful due to the nature of the environment. If we enter an environment in which many people have the flu, we may feel fortunate that we do not have the virus, but we must still be careful since the germs permeate the atmosphere. We are not simply addressing dysfunctional patterns from the past; we are also looking at ways to fortify and strengthen ourselves so that we will not acquire additional dysfunctional patterns in the future.

Question: If someone in your environment has a problem, how much do they affect you and the other people in the environment?

Answer: Just ask any householder or even any *brahmacari* or renunciate. If your roommate is angry, untidy, or stays up all night while you try to sleep, it will definitely affect you.

Similarly, when a man and woman live together, their anxieties, fears, distress, and happiness will constantly affect the other person to various extents. As a *brahmacari* or a householder, the condition of the person who you care about will affect you very directly. Any state of their mind such as anger or happiness will affect you because you share some similar space—physical, psychological, and spiritual. If you take your spiritual life very seriously but your partner abuses alcohol or does not read and chant, it will make your own *sadhana* much more difficult. On the other hand, if you both want to hear from the scriptures, when you come home from work, you can honor your meal together and then read, which will help both of you accelerate in spiritual life.

Question: Someone might be afraid to address the many different emotional scars that they carry not only from this lifetime but from many different lifetimes as well. What do you recommend for a person with this type of fear?

Answer: First of all, we really do not have to go back to previous lifetimes; we should simply understand that our past lives influence our current life. A person studying in a university does not necessarily need to go back to primary school but they realize that their previous education definitely has an effect on their present situation. In most cases, we can barely remember all the details from our childhood what to speak of previous lifetimes. However, we do have to deal with the many obstacles that influence us now, and, according to our ability, we can research certain outstanding experiences in this lifetime that have made impressions on us. After we identify these experiences, we can then try to address the issues.

For instance, we may wonder how we can advance if

we have to constantly think about all the different sixty-four offenses which Srila Rupa Gosvami explains in the *Bhakti-rasamrta-sindhu*. We can commit so many types of *aparadhas* or offenses such as offenses against the *guru*, the holy places of pilgrimage, the devotees, the holy name, and during service. Even if we try, we will not be able to analyze all these details. However, it is not our duty to get into such minute details and rules. We have the general principle, and by opening ourselves up, we will experience the benefits from the general principle. God comes in at this point. He is in the heart and is giving us knowledge, remembrance, and also forgetfulness. However, although the Supreme Lord gives us the knowledge, we still have to act. Krishna gave Arjuna the necessary instructions but Arjuna still had to make his own decision to act. Krishna gives us so many instructions about the dangers of the mind and the manifestation of lust in the body. He tells us to always think of Him but now we have to also decide how to act.

We should not just think that we will succeed through faith alone and then disregard works or effort. The mercy comes in association with effort. However, it is easier said than done; therefore, one should humbly pray, "Dear Krishna, this task is beyond me. Please help me and let me become a better servant." The materialists who try to use their own analytical abilities and function on their own strength will eventually get frustrated because, at some point, their own endeavors will simply not work out for them. Although we do not want to just depend on our own minute abilities, we also do not want to remove ourselves from action and just expect the mercy to somehow fall from the sky. For this reason, the *acaryas* give us many details. They teach us to recognize the nature of a *sadhu* so that we can become *sadhus* ourselves and take shelter of them. The scriptures constantly provide us with guidelines to check ourselves.

The idea is to develop a greater sense of humility. When we have more humility, these obstacles will no longer seem so difficult because we will really want to act properly and find ways to become better servants. Then, the Lord will guide us and give us more facilitation to deal with our issues. In some cases, God will guide us to a person who can help us, and we should see this help as His guidance.

Question: Thank you for discussing a subject that is so necessary for us to look at and strive to understand. My understanding of the quality of forgiveness is that it is necessary because it is a quality of the heart that allows us to approach the idea of love. We have come to a process that involves the highest love, but if we cannot embrace or understand the quality of forgiveness, we become stuck in the cycle of continuous reactions. By understanding this positive quality of forgiveness, we can really embrace the issues that seem to block us and accept the betrayals and attacks that have come into our lives. Simply because we have taken birth in this material world, these setbacks and attacks will happen, but when they happen, we should have the ability to apply forgiveness in that situation and dissipate the betrayal.

Answer: Living in the material world means that people will make mistakes (*bhrama*), fall into illusion (*pramada*), cheat others (*vipralipsa*), and possess imperfect senses (*karanapatava*). Sometimes we will find ourselves on the receiving end of some of those mistakes, illusions, or betrayals. We cannot fully avoid this fact. At some point, all people will experience these devastating experiences in some form. However, we must ask ourselves how long we will continue to fear the betrayal.

First of all, if we continue to carry it without forgiving, it means that we allow that person to constantly attack us again and again. Secondly, it means that we do not allow ourselves to move sufficiently into the present or future. Thirdly, it means that we are holding onto the duality, which will prevent us from transcending the problem. Finally, we cannot develop sufficient love or allow Krishna to be more active in our hearts if anger and grudges cover our hearts. We may even want the other person to also experience a betrayal or some type of pain. Then we need to ask ourselves how much pain we want the other person to experience before we can release them. We can look at the pastimes of the different *acaryas* in our line because many of them were also betrayed, disappointed, attacked, and misunderstood, but they did not harbor grudges or come down to that level.

We want to forgive others because we want to be forgiven. Just as we deal with people who have betrayed or disappointed us, we have also betrayed or disappointed people in our own lives. We also have hurt, wounded, or disappointed people; therefore, since we want to be forgiven, we want to forgive others. Finally, we must also forgive ourselves. Some people carry such unhealthy dialogues because they have made some bad choices or have gone through some bad events, but they will not forgive themselves. Consequently, they cannot move into a new aspect or chapter of their lives.

In a spiritual sense, it is just another way of playing God. We can play God in a grandiose mood by thinking ourselves to be wonderful like God Himself, or we can play the role of God through self-pity and lamentation so that we place the past and the wound in the center of our lives. Some people convert their wounds or mistakes into the enthroned deity in their minds and hearts. As long as these mistakes remain enthroned on the altar of our hearts, how will we allow God to enter? As we dethrone these other useless deities that have acted as substitutes for our connection with the divine, we will then have room for our real worshipful Deity, God. Remember that the greatest worship never just involves the externals; rather, it is the internal that accesses a deeper spirituality. Therefore, healthy internal dialogue is not optional; it is a necessity for a rich spiritual life.

Chapter 2

The Importance of Short-Term Goals

udarah sarva evaite
jnani tv atmaiva me matam
asthitah sa hi yuktatma
mam evanuttamam gatim

All these devotees are undoubtedly magnanimous souls, but he who is situated in knowledge of Me I consider to be just like My own self. Being engaged in My transcendental service, he is sure to attain Me, the highest and most perfect goal.
Bhagavad-gita 7.18

A Gradual Progression towards the Goal

Although we understand that a devotee ultimately wants to return to the spiritual world as an unalloyed servant of Krishna or God, we should also consider the importance of short-term goals as we gradually progress towards our ultimate goal. In the *Bhagavad-gita* 9.34, the Supreme Lord tells us the ultimate goal, which entails always thinking of Him:

> *man-mana bhava mad-bhakto*
> *mad-yaji mam namaskuru*
> *mam evaisyasi yuktvaivam*
> *atmanam mat-parayanah*

> Engage your mind always in thinking of Me, become My devotee, offer obeisances to Me and worship Me. Being completely absorbed in Me, surely you will come to Me.

The Lord directly tells us the ultimate goal of our existence. He tells us to always think of Him, never forget Him, and act in a way that will please Him. Ultimately, the *nitya-siddhas* or eternally liberated entities whose thoughts always remain perfectly aligned with God occupy this elevated platform.

Although most entities do not function on this particular level, the Supreme Lord does not reject them, considering them to be hopeless failures. Instead, in the twelfth chapter of the *Bhagavad-gita*, the Lord provides various alternatives for devotees who cannot always think of Him. He first recommends the process of *sadhana-bhakti* or devotional service in practice. We should engage in activities that will absorb the senses and mind in thoughts of the Supreme Personality of Godhead through the nine-fold process of devotional service.

> *sravanam kirtanam visnoh*
> *smaranam pada-sevanam*
> *arcanam vandanam dasyam*
> *sakhyam atma-nivedanam*
>
> Hearing and chanting about the transcendental holy name, form, qualities, paraphernalia and pastimes of Lord Visnu, remembering them, serving the lotus feet of the Lord, offering the Lord respectful worship with sixteen types of paraphernalia, offering prayers to the Lord, becoming His servant, considering the Lord one's best friend, and surrendering everything unto Him (in other words, serving Him with the body, mind and words) these nine processes are accepted as pure devotional service.
>
> Srimad-Bhagavatam 7.5.23

However, God knows that many souls cannot even practice these tenets of *bhakti*; therefore, He tells us to work for Him or help those who always follow the process of *sadhana-bhakti*. If we cannot always think of the Lord or follow the process of *sadhana-bhakti*, we should facilitate those who can follow the process by working for the Lord as a team player.

Even if we cannot work for God or help the practicing devotees, He still does not turn us away or consider us hopeless.

Rather, He tells us to do our own work to the best of our ability while remaining detached from the results. However, many people will even consider this last recommendation impossible or not want to follow due the nature of their desires; therefore, Krishna tells them to acquire knowledge. God Himself gives us these alternatives because although He ultimately tells us to think of Him, He understands that we may not be ready to fully absorb our minds on Him.

Constant meditation on God means that we will worship Him in full absorption and allow Him to work through us. At this stage, we will be fully in touch with the Lord due to the absence of the false ego, which manifests as fear, anger, envy, lust, greed, intoxication, madness, etc. The enemies of the mind will no longer attack us because we will always be in rapt meditation on God. All of these areas drag the mind away from the Lord because they pull it in other directions. Therefore, if we do not have the full ability to present our minds to God and receive Him in full, He gives us ways in which we can still gradually move towards Him and remain under His general care.

ye yatha mam prapadyante
tams tathaiva bhajamy aham
mama vartmanuvartante
manusyah partha sarvasah

As all surrender unto Me, I reward them accordingly. Everyone follows My path in all respects, O son of Prtha.
Bhagavad-gita 4.11

Whether we think of the Lord fully, engage in the other

processes, or simply resort to atheism or impersonalism, we still remain on the Lord's path and He reciprocates with us according to our thoughts and actions. We do not want to think myopically by categorizing a person who cannot work exclusively for God as a failure.

Practice Makes Perfect

If we look at some of the athletes who participate in the Olympic games, we will see that many of them have had intense goals for a long period of time. Many of them even began training as small children in order to excel in a particular discipline later in life. It is rare for a person to spontaneously decide overnight to excel in a field and develop proficiency through the process of osmosis. In most cases, a person must have serious determination to reach a goal and must practice very intensely. Sometimes these athletes have to practice every day for hours and hours. Their entire lives revolve around the particular activity. Although they may have other pursuits on the side, the sport constantly remains their major priority and they even center their diet, their friends, and their work upon swimming, track, skating, etc. In order to one day win the gold medal in the Olympics, these athletes need to regularly set short-term goals which will carry them to their ultimate goal.

Try to understand this point. If we just have long-term goals without any type of strategy or short-term goals, in most cases our ultimate goal will remain theoretical. We require intense meditation and strategies that can help us move from one success to another, until we finally reach the ultimate achievement. In the *Mahabharata* epic, why did Arjuna succeed in shooting the eye of a fish? Many powerful *ksatriyas* or warriors tried to pass this test in order to win Draupadi as their wife but only Arjuna could meet the challenge. Due to his intense training and ability to focus, he could reach that ultimate goal without any problem. His intense practice and gradual progression through specific short-term goals helped him attain a deep level of expertise.

A Ship without a Rudder

Although we see ourselves as worshippers of God and ultimately want to become fully God conscious, the mind is very strong. If we do not sufficiently plan, *maya*, Satan, or the temptation will plan for us. If we do not plan every day with short-term goals, it will become very hard to reach the ultimate goal. There is an African proverb that states, "If you do not know where you are going, any road will do." Even parents try to give their children certain goals that can guide them through their lives. Unfortunately, due to the increasing difficulties involved in child rearing these days, some parents simply allow their children to act as they please. The current educational system also tends to teach in this way by allowing the children to somewhat learn on their own. However, sending our children out into the world without some strategy or basic structure is comparable to sending a ship out to sea without its rudder. Under these circumstances, we will just send them away with a feeble hope that they will somehow gain some momentum. If we send them out without any facility, they can easily get stuck.

Obviously, the parents should recognize their children's individuality and try to inspire them according to their particular propensities because children will simply rebel if the parents try to force them to think, walk, or talk in a certain way at every single moment. However, if we send the children out into the world and allow them to act solely on their own feelings, not only will they end up like a ship without a rudder, but ultimately they will turn into obnoxious entities who even hate their parents for giving them that so-called freedom. They may later categorize that leniency as a lack of love or care since the parents have not used their resources to plan for their future.

A Means to Reach the End

The children or young members of spiritual societies hear year after year that our ultimate goal is to become pure devotees of the Lord. At the same time, they see so many deviations as well as sense gratification around them and feel bored by this ultimate goal that seems so far away and ambiguous. However, if some of these children have short-term goals that can absorb their energies, they will feel much more comfortable as they pass year after year in the devotional culture while simultaneously trying to embrace the ultimate goal. They need to feel some excitement, adventure, and achievement that can carry them throughout their lives.

I am passionately addressing this topic because I see what is happening in many environments and what is happening to myself. When I look back over the years, I understand that my spiritual mentor's mercy has kept me serving enthusiastically year after year, but I can also see how my short-term goals have played an important role. We constantly hear the word surrender but surrender is a process. Sometimes people tell us, "Just do your duty." However, *dharma* or religious duty is also based on capacity or *adhikara*. We cannot impose *dharma* on people but must inspire people to live by *dharma*. By honoring *dharma*, we position ourselves to naturally embrace *sanatana-dharma* or our eternal duty. If you just serve out of duty without any sense of excitement, gradually your life will become a disappointment and you will also consider yourself to be a disappointment to those who care for you most. Certain anxieties will continuously manifest in different ways, which simply stem from your lack of excitement in your life.

One way or the other, we are always crazy. Either we are crazy and intoxicated by love of God or we are just crazy about some type of sense gratification. It is just a matter of how we direct that intense craziness. As we develop a passion for certain goals according to our propensities, we will even begin to energize each other about our own particular concerns and interests. Conversely, if we just act mechanically or even grudgingly on a day-to-day basis, we will also begin to weaken the people around us because that lack of enthusiasm will gradually seep into everyone's consciousness and weaken our desire to honor particular goals.

For this reason, sometimes in the Olympic games, members of the same country will win the gold, silver, and bronze medals in one particular sport. Since the gold medalist practiced the sport with such passion, his or her enthusiasm raised the standards of the other athletes. Therefore, they have a whole team of powerful achievers due to a single person who could encourage others to reach higher levels of excellence through his or her own example.

If we only hear about the higher goal but do not have the strategy to reach that end, we will become almost like a cult. Since we will not have reached the higher goal, we will feel intimidated and we may even pretend that we have reached that point. Consequently, we will have people who desire to act or serve in their own way but will avoid these short-term goals since they do not want to seem independent. People might say, "You are just in *maya* or illusion. Don't try to be so independent. Just work." However, we do have certain abilities and tendencies that we can use in the service of *guru*, God, and the community. We should, if possible, engage in activities that are more suited to our natures, which is not *maya*, especially if we are following the nine-fold process. The Lord Himself gives us alternative ways to progress even if we cannot always think of Him. He gives us bona fide short-term goals. We do not want to connect with inauthentic short-term goals or ultimate goals, nor do we want to minimize the dynamic nature of Krishna consciousness. God is always active, and, as we find ways to harness our minds and ways to serve Him, our appreciation for the Lord will increase.

Evaluate the Goal

In order to avoid pursuing inauthentic goals or goals that we have no desire to reach, we must first identify which goal we want to seek in our lives and then identify the process which can help us reach that goal. If we want to make a quick evaluation of any teaching or philosophy, we can ask this simple but significant question: **What is the ultimate goal that a person can attain if he or she properly follows this process?** Every theology, philosophy, or religion has some specific goal that people can attain if they reach perfection in that process. Whether one wants to create heaven on earth; experience the energies of the Lord; develop certain *saktis* or mystic powers; go to paradise; or go to Vrndavana, the spiritual world, each process has specific requirements. Most importantly, the aspirant must have a certain consciousness associated with the desired goal in order to reach that end.

Sometimes people ask, "Do not all theologies and philosophies lead to the same goal?" If we carefully look at the goals of various processes, we may discover that they do in fact offer different goals and destinations. Why would a person study in a university for one type of degree and then expect to get another degree at the end? If a person wants certification in a particular area and sufficiently passes the courses, he or she will receive a degree according to that particular discipline. Considering this fact, a person should make the proper inquiries before entering into a discipline by asking, "What degree can I receive if I pass all of the courses in this particular area of study?" Just as we make these evaluations in academia and in other aspects of material life, we should certainly make this important evaluation in spiritual life.

Some people might even feel shocked and uncomfortable when they find out the goal of their particular alignment. However, if the goal suits them, they should ask a second question: **What do I need to do to acquire this goal?** Even if some people are not ready to fully embrace the necessary rules and regulations, the mere recognition of such requirements can help them move in the proper direction. At least they will keep the ultimate goal in mind in spite of their inability to fully adopt all of the practices. In this case, the person can do the best that they can in order to come as close to that goal as possible. However, if they do not want that goal, they should involve themselves in another system that will help them acquire their desired goal.

If the person does want the goal and can follow the process to a certain degree, he or she should ask a third question: **Have the serious followers of the process attained the goal, and,**

if so, what have they achieved? We should study the people who have already reached the goal because, ultimately, we will expect to have similar experiences and qualities when we attain the goal. If we find a goal that suits us but do not have the capacity to follow the process, we need to understand that we will not reach the goal until we can properly follow the practices. If we really do want a certain goal, it means that in time we will try to position ourselves to follow all the necessary requirements. On the other hand, if we do not want to do the necessary, we really need to honestly ask ourselves if we actually want that goal. In some cases, we may not want the ultimate goal and should honestly find a different path to follow along with its necessary practices. However, we may never want to take all the necessary steps to acquire a certain goal, which means that we should find a process that we can follow and then pursue that goal genuinely.

Find a Project

After understanding the type of goal we wish to pursue, we want to strategize and find ways to maintain our enthusiasm. If we examine our lives, we will discover that we feel happiest in our spiritual journey when we fully absorb our minds in a project or plan as an offering. We may serve in so many various ways, but as we meditate on our offering while remembering our position as devotees, we will have the ability to harness the mind. I find that when I do not focus my mind on a specific goal, my mind becomes crazy or goes all over the place. This constant fluctuation can cause one to feel very insignificant, depressed, angry, or lonely because the mind has this tendency.

At times, when you do have a plan or goal that enthuses you, it will energize you to the point that you accomplish far more. Each person's project will differ. For instance, a devotee in a temple or monastic environment may ask, "What is the goal for a person living in the temple who does not have a spouse or children and simply engages in monastic services?" In this case, the goal may not deal directly with the material energy but may revolve around the person's daily services. For example, the devotee can decide to read volumes of scriptures in a period of six months or try to organize various improvements for the monastery and for his or her personal life by the end of the year. We should select a goal in which we can place all of our energies. In this way, we will feel more excited about the spiritual journey because we will have the means to work towards this goal on a daily basis. It is too dangerous to just let the mind loose. Since our mind and our environments constantly challenge and threaten us, we have to remain alert and develop more power within ourselves if we want to have the ability to reach the ultimate goal.

We need to examine our lives more closely. When you are planning for events and projects, life becomes much richer for you. However, notice the effects on the mind when you simply move through the daily rituals. Although you may live in or visit the temple, monastery, church, mosque, or synagogue for worship, you will not feel happy unless you can identify with particular pursuits that you want to accomplish as a part of your life. Considering the power of the mind, we somewhat have to trick it in order to engage it in the devotional culture. If we do not engage it, it will engage us.

Once, when I was part of a special program involved in distributing my spiritual master's books to museums, libraries, universities, and professors, our team went to our spiritual mentor with our pens and pencils in order to get very specific instructions on how to distribute his books. We were prepared to receive very specific and elaborate instructions that would help us reach our goal. However, my spiritual mentor simply told us, "Just do your best and Krishna will help you." At times when we receive a general instruction, we have the responsibility to imbibe it and apply it specifically to our particular goal. Although the instruction may seem simple or general, if it is an empowered instruction and we accept it, we will attain great success. Our team accepted this simple instruction and we later obtained success beyond our imagination. We had several creative, intelligent men on our team so we each set short-term goals and strategies to facilitate us in accomplishing longer-term goals.

Just take some time to examine your own propensities in order to discover the activities that enthuse you. As a devotee, what enlivens and excites you in your spiritual practices? By pushing yourself in certain ways to achieve these personal goals, you will feel happier. Once again, put the book away for a day and write down some of your short-term personal goals and your plans to accomplish them.

Rules and Regulations Necessary but Secondary

Under the system of *varnasrama-dharma* or the Vedic social system meant to help people elevate their collective and individual consciousness, people will have different abilities and idiosyncratic tendencies but each person can be encouraged to serve according to their propensities. Although we can make an offering to the Supreme Lord according to our type of work (*varna*) and our spiritual order of life (*asrama*), we ultimately understand that all *varnas* and *asramas* are secondary and are simply the means to reach a higher level.

Nevertheless, the system of *varnasrama-dharma* is still a reality and part of the field of activities in which one may make offerings to God. The great saints ultimately tell us, *aham brahmasmi*, which emphasizes that our eternal identity far surpasses these bodies. Love is not bound by any of these particular designations since it is far beyond all of these categories. However, these divisions can assist us in our progress and act as short-term goals. For instance, if someone genuinely tries to serve the Lord from the mode of ignorance, gradually he or she will accelerate to the mode of passion and then to the mode of goodness. Sometimes we act in the different modes at different times, but if we try our best with determination, there will be a natural graduation.

The Supreme Personality of Godhead tells us that everyone is on His path and He also tells us to just engage in His service in spite of our desires.

*akamah sarva-kamo va
moksa-kama udara-dhih
tivrena bhakti-yogena
yajeta purusam param*

> Whether one is without desire [the condition of the devotees], or is desirous of all fruitive results, or is after liberation, one should with all efforts try to worship the Supreme Personality of Godhead for complete perfection, culminating in Krishna consciousness.
> *Srimad-Bhagavatam* 2.3.10

Even if we have numerous material desires or just desire liberation, the *Bhagavatam* still tells us to go to the Lord. Of course, God initially tells us to approach Him in a certain way but He then makes certain arrangements to facilitate us in our growth. For instance, if a teacher gives a lesson that the student cannot understand, she may then make another arrangement to teach the student. However, the teacher must always keep her ultimate goal in the forefront because she does want her student to eventually graduate. Similarly, we must always remember the ultimate goal; otherwise, in the process of working for the Lord or acquiring knowledge, we may begin to consider the work or the knowledge to be the ultimate goal.

The Supreme Lord is definitely asking for something far beyond these external activities but He is also giving us alternatives. If we begin to think that the Lord only cares about these rules and regulations, we will serve mechanically or with a hard heart and forget that Krishna really wants us to always think of Him. We engage in these activities so that we can lovingly think of Him, ultimately developing pure, unalloyed devotion. Text Two of *The Nectar of Instruction* explains that too much attachment to the rules and regulations can also cause a fall down:

atyaharah prayasas ca
prajalpo niyamagrahah
jana-sangas ca laulyam ca
sadbhir bhaktir vinasyati

One's devotional service is spoiled when he becomes too entangled in the following six activities: (1) eating more than necessary or collecting more funds than required; (2) over-endeavoring for mundane things that are very difficult to obtain; (3) talking unnecessarily about mundane subject matters; (4) practicing the scriptural rules and regulations only for the sake of following them and not for the sake of spiritual advancement, or rejecting the rules and regulations of the scriptures and working independently or whimsically; (5) associating with worldly-minded persons who are not interested in Krishna consciousness; and (6) being greedy for mundane achievements.[3]

In this discussion, we will give special attention to number four. We should not consider that Krishna only wants us to follow rules nor should we minimize them; rather, we should honor them as a prerequisite to the process of devotional service while simultaneously trying to improve on the quality of our mental culture.

Small Achievements Increase Enthusiasm

We really need to acknowledge the seriousness of our position in this material body and in this material world. As residents in *maya's* camp, the general mental culture will constantly try to keep us entangled in the material energy unless we develop ways to sufficiently harness the mind. For this reason, Bhaktivinoda Thakura, a great Vaisnava saint, explains that unless a person is a *paramahamsa* or a completely pure saint, the mind must have a certain amount of satisfying stimulation. We must engage the mind in such a way that we feel good about our services, our environment, the process, and ourselves. We cannot just work indefinitely without some *ruci* or spiritual taste. We can join a religious institution or spiritual community and temporarily function according to the instructions of the authorities, but if we somehow fail to develop this taste or do not have a chance to work on our own personal goals while striving for the ultimate goal, we will undergo various disturbances.

We are not implying that everyone should act according to their own desires and consider this anarchic arrangement to be spiritual life because this mood has brought down ultimate spiritual culture and created religious superficiality. Krishna tells us to always think of Him, and if we cannot always meditate on Him, He gives us alternatives. However, He does not remove the ultimate goal or leave us with ambiguous short-term goals. He clearly states in the *Bhagavad-gita* that we should always think of Him, and if we cannot engage in this exclusive meditation, He tells us to practice devotional service. If we cannot even practice *sadhana-bhakti*, He tells us to work for Him or encourage those who work for Him. Our next option is to meditate or acquire knowledge. He gave us these short-term goals to help us progress towards the ultimate goal.

Often, when devotees engage in devotional service without the specific means to reach the end, eventually they walk around like zombies or they begin to consider the spiritual journey to be impossible or impractical. As we reach short-term goals, we will feel more enthusiastic to reach the next goal and ultimately the final goal. The progression through short-term goals encouraged many Olympic athletes to continue their pursuit towards the gold medal. Eventually they began to think, "I want to be the best in the world, and through my practice and training, I know that I can possibly reach this goal." Even if they do not immediately win the gold medal but receive the silver, it will encourage them to try harder for their next competition. As they see their goal manifesting, they will try even harder to remain focused.

Similarly, as we acquire a short-term goal, it will help to absorb our minds and focus our energies. Seeing the goal unfold may even strengthen our faith and give us pleasure according to our own particular propensity or idiosyncratic tendency. This enthusiasm can help us in our endeavor to always think of the Supreme Mother-Father God and offer everything to Them. We never want to neglect love of Godhead and *saranagati* or full surrender, which we accept as our ultimate goal. Although it is dangerous to minimize or reject the final goal, it is just as dangerous to neglect our short-term goals because doing so will lead us into stagnation. If we think of the ultimate goal as impossible, we will be defeated from the start. We will begin to rationalize our deviations and accept mediocrity while doubting the entire process. On the other hand, if we do not succeed in our short-term goals or fail to harness our minds and senses in a positive way, they will become overly active. If we have no enthusiasm for any type of devotional engagement, we will develop enthusiasm for sense gratification.

Why did Srila Rupa Gosvami, the great Vedic scholar and renunciate, emphasize *utsaha* or enthusiasm as foremost? If we lack enthusiasm, we will begin to settle back into the mindsets that we have carried with us from many previous lifetimes when our senses and environments entirely enslaved us. Most importantly, we must recognize the importance of *sraddha* or faith in our endeavor to break through the modes of material nature. This task requires an intense focus that does not just develop perfectly overnight. If it does develop quickly in a person, in some cases the individual has come into this life with a very high level of *adhikara* or devotional assets from previous lifetimes. It means that he or she has already engaged in so many spiritual practices in order to reach this particular point.

While we keep the ultimate goal of full God consciousness in mind, we want to encourage each other to look closer at our daily lives and examine certain goals that we want to achieve according to our *varna, asrama,* and particular idiosyncratic propensities. We want to find some specific goals that we can feel happy to offer to the community, to the mission, to our families, and to ourselves. By this endeavor, *maya* will not hunt us or assault us to the same extent because our spiritual pursuits will occupy our minds and enthuse us. Each person must examine their own nature in order to recognize their capabilities along with the activities that inspire or enthuse them. In this way, they can continue in their devotional service in pursuit of the ultimate goal.

Resolute Determination

The Vedic scriptures mainly refer to the ultimate goal because we must always keep that final goal in mind. However, we must realize that the Lord gave us the *varnasrama-dharma* system and He also gave us methods to continue on the spiritual path even if we cannot always think of Him. We need to constantly remind ourselves of the ultimate goal and never minimize the necessity to reach that goal. We can honestly reach that goal through our integral successes and achievements, which move us closer to our ultimate achievement.

Krishna says in *Bhagavad-gita* 2.41:

> *vyavasayatmika buddhir*
> *ekeha kuru-nandana*
> *bahu-sakha hy anantas ca*
> *buddhayo 'vyavasayinam*
>
> Those who are on this path are resolute in purpose, and their aim is one. O beloved child of the Kurus, the intelligence of those who are irresolute is many-branched.

Those on this path have one ultimate goal; that is, to develop pure love of God and return to the spiritual kingdom. On the other hand, the environment and *maya* will quickly enslave a person with irresolute intelligence and drag them in many directions. However, if we have a specific direction, the mind will not fall prey to the enticements. The purport to this verse from the *Bhagavad-gita* says:

> A strong faith that by Krishna consciousness one will be elevated to the highest perfection of life is called *vyavasayatmika* intelligence. The *Caitanya-caritamrta* (*Madhya* 22.62) states:
>
> *'sraddha'-sabde – visvasa kahe sudrdha niscaya*
> *krsne bhakti kaile sarva-karma krta haya*

The Importance of Short-Term Goals 65

> Faith means unflinching trust in something sublime. When one is engaged in the duties of Krishna consciousness, he need not act in relationship to the material world with obligations to family traditions, humanity or nationality. Fruitive activities are the engagements of one's reactions from past good or bad deeds. When one is awake in Krishna consciousness, he need no longer endeavor for good results in his activities. When one is situated in Krishna consciousness, all activities are on the absolute plane, for they are no longer subject to dualities like good and bad. The highest perfection of Krishna consciousness is renunciation of the material conception of life. This state is automatically achieved by progressive Krishna consciousness.[4]

We have the goal but it is achieved through progressive achievements and successes that increase our faith, determination, and enthusiasm. We do not want to bewilder anyone through this discussion because we in no way want to propagate relativism. We clearly have an ultimate *siddhanta* or goal. However, we acquire that goal through each achievement and we want to creatively use our minds to find ways to give more of ourselves to the Supreme Lord each day. **The progression through short-term goals will keep us enthused and on track toward accomplishing our long-term goal.**

The Guru and the Disciple

Some might have heard the story of the disciple who eagerly wanted self-realization. This disciple earnestly tried to follow all the necessary requirements of a good disciple, but somehow or other, he did not seem to develop any realization. From time to time, he would intensely inquire from his *guru* and complain about his situation. He wanted to know when he would be able to attain self-realization and how he would reach this goal. However, the spiritual master did not seem to acknowledge his bewilderment. He practically did not even respond.

One day, the disciple and the *guru* took a walk by the river. The spiritual master walked the disciple into the river and then with full force he suddenly pushed the disciple's head into the water, practically drowning the boy. The disciple must have felt completely shocked and disturbed, especially since the *guru* is supposed to be the major source of solace and love for the disciple. However, his *guru* suddenly submerged his head in water in a seemingly strange attempt to drown him. As the disciple's life air gradually decreased, he only thought of ways to pull his head above the surface of the water for a breath of air.

Just before the disciple gave up the body, the spiritual master finally released his head from under the water. In a very grave but caring tone, the *guru* explained, "When I held your head under the water, you solely thought of ways to obtain air. Your entire consciousness focused only on this one purpose and every aspect of your dwindling existence strove for survival or liberation. When you develop this same kind of pinpointed intensity for the development of love of God, irrespective of other distractions, only then will you attain self-realization. When you have such intense desperation and desire for God's love and mercy, then you will reach this ultimate goal."

Questions and Answers

Question: I recently discovered that I really need to find some project that enthuses me. When I attended a seminar last Monday, a man discussed an incident at his work with us. His fellow employee had a problem so the man asked him, "What is it that really makes you happy in life? What enthuses you?" At that point, the employee started to cry because nobody had ever asked him that question before. I wanted to give this example because I see the same thing happening in some of our lives. We often become so involved in our daily duties that we never really ask these deeper questions. What makes me want to wake up in the morning and approach the day enthusiastically instead of just mechanically fulfilling my duties? At this point, I really want to understand this on a personal level because I want to give. I think we all ultimately want to give our all in Krishna consciousness but we will not really function in this way unless we really enjoy our services.

I even have the same experience with children. In order to really bring the best out of children, especially in terms of education, they need to have a vested interest in the subject matter. They have to want to learn or engage in the activity. Then you will not even need to discipline or shout at them because they will want to do it automatically. Since I have never thought about this before, I want to really take the time for introspection. What really inspires me the most in my spiritual quest? Thank you for presenting this topic. You always have such a radical, universal, personal, caring, and loving spiritual presentation.

Answer: Thank you. I am an insignificant person, but I try to see people, especially those who are committed to pursuing transcendence, as most significant. You made a good point. If we just continue to work and work without really examining the deeper reflections in the mind and consciousness, we will eventually have problems. Unless we develop *ruci* or spiritual taste, we will develop taste for engagements outside the boundaries of Krishna consciousness. For instance, some of you may find it hard to deeply absorb yourselves in the books; however, when you have to give a *Srimad-Bhagavatam* or *Bhagavad-gita* class, you will become absorbed in the books on a deeper level. Then you will get more out of the scriptures because you will have to share your understanding of the material. Since you have set a goal to give class, you have put your mind in a situation that will harness it and force it to be more attentive and accountable. Simply by reading the books without the pressure of an impending class, you may not internalize as much of the material.

Children always provide a good example. We can even think back to our own childhood and to the times when we actually enjoyed a subject matter or class. Some of you might have enjoyed art, and when the bell rang for the class to begin, you just felt excitement and enthusiasm. You fully exerted yourself in art class because you felt happy. However, if you had to go to math or history class, it was like death. Sitting in that room and hearing the teacher's monotone voice seemed to last forever. In such situations, even if you managed to get a good grade, you did not really learn much. You may have simply forced yourself to memorize dates and facts. We all know that we will absorb ourselves more in an activity that excites us and we will consequently give more to the community and to ourselves.

Question: Your example of children in school brought up a question. Although we may not like history, we may still have to pass that class. How do we develop enough enthusiasm for a subject matter that we need to pass?

Answer: We can use this same example to answer your question. Some teenagers drop out of school because the subjects bore them but other teenagers may stay in school in spite of these boring subjects because they have other areas of interest to pursue. Since some of their classes or extracurricular activities excite them, they stay in school and graduate. People will never like all of the things that they must deal with or learn, but if they cannot find some areas that enthuse them, they will have problems. A *brahmana* or a scholarly priest may find it difficult to clean the yard and wash the pots, but because he has other goals that interest him, he will wash the pots nicely so that he can have time for the activities that he really enjoys. If this *brahmana* washes the dishes very nicely and efficiently, he can then go upstairs and spend four hours reading and learning *mantras* or prayers. The danger arises when a person does not have any enthusiasm for any of these activities because he or she will then run to the disco, take intoxications, or fall into some other type of sense gratification.

Question: I appreciated your example of the athlete who must set little goals in order to reach the big goal. I often concern myself mainly with big projects that become so overwhelming that I simply push the small achievements to the side. Although I execute my duty, I find that I do not feel the sweetness. I even end up feeling bad when I cannot reach such a big goal. Thank you for this class because I think that it will help me break down my goals on a daily basis so that I can take some realistic steps towards the attainments of the larger goals.

Answer: This is a very good example. We can have such big goals hanging over our heads that they may even cause us to feel like failures. The ultimate goal may seem so distant that we lose our self-esteem or experience depression, anxiety, and gloom. It will even minimize our actual ability to achieve and cause us to feel such anxiety about the goal that we will give up the struggle. Eventually, we will even lose the confidence that we can attain the goal. Again, we can see the importance of short-term goals. In one sense, anyone can perform all types of miracles and amazing feats if God wants us to, but we often stop ourselves from achieving these higher levels due to fear, weak association, lack of faith, and a lack of planning. However, even if we have small achievements and successes, these small steps will open us up to greater possibilities.

There is a whole movement among athletes now to break previous records and perform superhuman feats that no one could surpass one or two decades ago. Although the body has limits, every year athletes continue to break these records. Now coaches are paying psychologists and sports trainers millions of dollars to train athletes in a mental culture that deals with visualization and to encourage them to embrace the mood of success. As the athletes own that mood, it can carry them from one successful experience to the other. These trainers want the athletes to recognize their accomplishments so that they can accomplish more and more. Many of the winners have a stronger mental culture than their opponents. Often they have similar athletic abilities, which means that success depends on the athlete with the stronger mental culture.

Similarly, in our *mana-seva* or mental worship, the contemplations of the mind will have a significant influence on our fate. For this reason, at a certain level in our devotional service and devotional maturity, we may engage in the reflections on our eternal engagements in the spiritual world even while we remain in our physical bodies. Of course, devotees must have bona fide guidance in these areas. At a certain level of advancement, they may receive blessings and understand their original identity in the spiritual world. They will begin to interact with and reflect on the spiritual environment so that it becomes a greater part of their essence. Eventually, it will become their total essence. This is the power of the mind when it becomes our friend, and also its danger when it turns into our enemy.

Question: It seems that our goal is somewhat more intangible on a material level than the gold medal in the Olympic games. For instance, I just read that we should meditate on the third *sloka* from the *Siksastaka*, which states that we should be more humble than the straw in the street and more tolerant than a tree. We should give all respect to others without expecting any respect for ourselves. This mindset is difficult to capture and, in some ways, I feel almost fearful of success since it may go to my head. I see it happening to people on the spiritual path. Can you give some short-term goals that move in the direction of our ultimate, intangible goal?

Answer: Consider the last *sloka* of the *Sri Siksastaka*:

> *aslisya va pada-ratam pinastu mam*
> *adarsanan marma-hatam karotu va*
> *yatha tatha va vidadhatu lampato*
> *mat-prana-nathas tu sa eva naparah*

> I know no one but Krishna as my Lord, and He shall remain so even if He handles me roughly by His embrace or

> makes me brokenhearted by not being present before me. He is completely free to do anything and everything, for He is always my worshipful Lord, unconditionally.

This is a pretty intense goal. However, we understand that we gradually want to move in this direction.

Your point is profound because people are not only afraid of failure but they are also afraid of success. The subconscious mind is more powerful than the conscious mind. Although we might consciously speak and act in a certain way, if the subconscious mind continues to say 'no', it will win over. We talked about this in our discussion on the internal dialogue. There are people and even devotees who fail or run away from a goal because they are afraid of success or afraid of what it may mean. However, if we think more in terms of short-term goals as well as long-term goals, we will have less fear because we will focus on achievements that make us happy. In this way, we do not have to feel overly anxious about its implications later; rather, we can just work progressively until we have the ability to reach that bigger goal.

Although many different complexities and difficulties may confront us in this process, we must remember that the process is actually very simple. It depends on the activities in the mind. We want to gradually turn our mind into the deepest lover without fear of distraction from the different allurements or even fear of loving deeply. This is the duty of the spiritual warrior. Whether we have money or not, whether we have good health or not, or whether we have a big project or a simple service, we want to feel eager to receive God's loving embrace. Whatever is happening in our lives, we want to remind ourselves that

The Importance of Short-Term Goals 73

Krishna has picked us up after so many lifetimes in order to bring us to this point in this lifetime. If we can just develop the proper mental culture, the last layers will fall away and Krishna, who is constantly reaching out for us, will feel happy to see us approach Him. He will hope that we do not lose our determination at this point.

Even though we have so much to do, we need to stop creating more complications than necessary. We have to realize that God consciousness involves more than just building big projects, memorizing numerous verses, or organizing big campaigns, festivals and so on. These activities alone will not give us pure love of God. We actually already have a connection with the Lord, but, in order to realize this fact, we need to get rid of the illusion. As we begin to develop some sanity through our short-term goals, we will gradually understand that we already have the ultimate goal that we simply need to rediscover.

We want to discuss these issues as a way to help ourselves in spite of the increasing difficulties in the environment. The culture of confusion and fear is pervading the entire planet at this time. Due to the changes in the government and the economy, people's fear and confusion will continue to accelerate and allow *maya* to penetrate more all over the planet. In order to replace or counteract the fear and bewilderment, we need a greater sense of love. In one sense, there is only love and fear. As we harness the mind more carefully, we will exhibit more of our love because we will feel happy about who we are and who we are becoming. Then we will experience more of the great excitement and adventure involved in developing our full God consciousness. However, when we do not harness the mind sufficiently, the tapes and music from previous lifetimes and even from this life will just start playing over and over again. If the subconscious mind has a deeper connection with these old tapes in spite of our external activities, these old tapes will zap us and this noise will simply overcome us.

One day when we return to the spiritual world, we will look back at ourselves and realize that it was worth the struggle. Although the struggles seem so difficult, if not impossible, while we suffer through them, one day we will see the simplicity. We simply have to position ourselves in the proper way to receive the help that is always accessible. Material time may seem excessively long, but, in relation to time in the spiritual world, it is actually very short. It will seem that our absence from our eternal home lasted for only a few days. We considered the time to be long and the task to be impossible but, when it ends, it will seem just like a bad nightmare. As we keep pursuing the long-term goal of reuniting with the Supreme Lord in the spiritual world, each short-term goal that we accomplish brings us more genuinely closer to our ultimate goal. Small victories aggregate eventually to total victory. Keep marching on spiritual warriors for ultimate victory is in sight!

Chapter 3

An Attitude of Gratitude

*tam sukharadhyam rjubhir
ananya-saranair nrbhih
krtajnah ko na seveta
duraradhyam asadhubhih*

What grateful soul is there who would not render his loving service to such a great master as the Personality of Godhead? The Lord can be easily pleased by spotless devotees who resort exclusively to Him for protection, though the unrighteous man finds it difficult to propitiate Him.
Srimad-Bhagavatam 3.19.36

Everything Rests Upon the Lord

When we have a mindset of impoverishment and fear, and do not appreciate that the Supreme Personality of Godhead either directly or indirectly arranges everything, it distracts from our ability to progress and takes away from our physical and mental sense of well-being. Such an unhealthy mental state may even lead to failure and bring many negative situations into our lives. For these reasons, we want to present this conception of gratitude since it can counteract many of these destructive mindsets. The attitude of gratitude develops through the understanding that everything rests upon the Lord.

mattah parataram nanyat
kincid asti dhananjaya
mayi sarvam idam protam
sutre mani-gana iva

O conqueror of wealth, there is no truth superior to Me. Everything rests upon Me, as pearls are strung on a thread.
Bhagavad-gita 7.7

If we really understand that all things rest upon the Supreme Personality of Godhead, we will then try to use every circumstance in our life for growth. We can look closer at every situation in order to discover the message or lesson that we can learn. It can help us find ways to serve better or learn more about other people, the environment, and ourselves. It can also help us appreciate the power and mercy of the Lord, and understand the ways in which *maya* influences us so that we can get around such obstacles. Gratitude is a valuable way to take care of our physical, mental, and spiritual states.

What Blocks the Development of Gratitude

The Enemies of the Mind

The enemies of the mind such as fear, anxiety, anger, grief, depression, illusion, envy, and jealousy will naturally hinder our ability to develop gratitude because we will only focus on our own challenges or expectations. Fear indicates that we are not appreciating the present or the past but are in too much anxiety about the future. If we allow the illusions to capture us, we will not see or experience the divinity all around us. For instance, the false ego may sometimes cause a person to think solely about him or herself and develop such illusions of grandeur that he or she cannot appreciate others or see God as the greatest personality. On the other hand, a person's insecurities or inferiority complexes can also inhibit proper gratitude. This person might receive so much assistance from other people and even from God, but he will not access gratitude because his low self-esteem will prevent him from seeing and identifying with these positive situations in his life. In other words, such a person simply cannot see the world around him or her and consequently remains unappreciative.

In other cases, some people may never express any gratitude in spite of your endeavors to serve or assist them. Many people these days never even say "thank you." Sometimes they will not say "thank you" because they feel that they deserve whatever comes to them and expect even more to come. Other people do not express their gratitude because they simply are not aware of what you have done or what others have done for them. They cannot appreciate or respect what comes to them because their low self-esteem prevents them from attuning themselves to the kindness directed toward them.

Lack of Thankfulness

As spiritualists, we should always be in the spirit of "thank you." As we interact with people, we should always think and say, "Thank you. Thank you for helping me to see my own envious nature. Thank you for helping me look closer at my own ego. Thank you for helping me look closer at my own selfishness. Thank you for helping me to understand how I can act as a better parent. Thank you for showing me the need to become a better disciple. Thank you for helping me to find ways to preach more effectively. Thank you for helping me to understand that every situation is an opportunity to serve and glorify the Lord. Thank you for setting a good example."

When we do not genuinely say thank you in our lives, this ungrateful attitude will interfere with our spiritual growth. Sometimes we simply must come to such a level of gratitude that we can just say, "Thank you Lord for allowing me to be sick and giving me this opportunity to read more. Thank you for this opportunity to be more introspective. Thank you for giving me this chance to appreciate health and use it more efficiently when I have it." When someone criticizes us, we can thank them for helping us look closer at ourselves. When someone praises us, we can thank the Lord for showing us our big egos and thank Him for seeing that it needs to be deflated. When we face dishonor, we can thank the Lord for keeping us humble and preventing us from relying entirely on our own abilities. We want to have gratitude towards the Lord, towards His representatives, and towards everyone in our environment. We can even feel grateful for those who have fallen into *maya* for distinctly showing us what we want to avoid.

Excessive False Ego

When we have too much false ego, we will definitely not

appreciate the behavior of other people when they set good examples. Consequently, when they help us look closer at ourselves, we will simply try to hide or fall into a defensive mode. However, if we are evolving spiritually, situations and events will happen in our lives that will allow us to see our own progression and feel grateful. Genuine spiritual advancement will naturally humble us because we will understand that such progression is beyond our own means. The great ecstasy that we begin to experience will then humble us even more. Although such experiences will cause us to feel unworthy, we will feel eager to have more. By allowing the Lord to work through us, more positive changes will happen and we will feel constant anticipation as we wait for the next experience and the next adventure.

People who constantly feel sad, depressed, anxious, and disturbed will rarely have a genuine sense of gratitude, even in spiritual communities. Some people only see the negative aspects of any situation due to low self-esteem, false ego, cynicism, or a faultfinding mindset; consequently, they miss the basic beautiful realities. Often people just search for the faults like a rat that just connects with unhealthy or filthy situations. Due to some of these negative mindsets, some people only look for the negative, and when they find it, they hold onto it tenaciously. Then people begin to wonder why they feel so unfulfilled and unhappy around others. Nevertheless, in spite of their emptiness, even when they have the association of other people, they will still only consider their own plan, idea, or particular material pleasures. Even neophyte spiritualists will sometimes fall into this mentality and only meditate on the fulfillment of their own wants and needs. However, this is not a mature spiritual warrior because true spiritualists practically never think only about themselves.

What Supports Gratitude

Selflessness

In the higher spiritual realms, thinking solely of oneself is inimical to loving exchanges. Love never just revolves around the desires, needs, or experiences of the individual. Rather, the individual actually searches for some type of service to offer to the beloved and specifically wants to know the best way to offer that service. Not only will the person endeavor to nicely render service, but he or she will also look closely at the beloved to see if that type of service actually satisfies the person. If not, the individual is immediately ready to make a shift in order to do whatever pleases the beloved. However, some people do not love. They do not love themselves or others; therefore, they have utilitarian and opportunistic reflections. In most cases, it simply turns into anger because they feel so disturbed that others interfere with their particular plan. In the material world, people form parties, clubs, groups, alliances, and even marriages with the idea that the other person or group of people will help to fulfill their own desires. Consequently, people will simply remain miserable because love does not come out of selfishness; rather, selfishness blocks love. I discuss this topic in detail in my book, *Spiritual Warrior II: Transforming Lust into Love*.

As we genuinely honor the arrangements that God has already made, gratitude will naturally form an intricate part of that reflection. Gratitude also involves the appreciation of what other people have already done for you. By maintaining such reflections, you will then live and imbibe so much happiness in life. Gratitude does not develop by carrying around so much anxiety from the past, which we then drag into the present and future. Actually, it involves learning from the past in spite of the difficulties and looking at the future in order to find ways to grow. We should constantly try to find more ways to reflect on the Lord, and praise Him and His devotees. When we think too much about ourselves, we will disturb others or we will have emotional, psychological, and physiological problems that will make our spiritual acceleration more complex. By increasingly honoring life as it appears in many, many forms and trying to see the Krishna or God factor in all situations, a devotee will advance much faster and will have a more genuine sense of spiritual maturity. A symptom of advancement is that a devotee will not play into the duality as much.

Recognizing the Meaning in Life

There is a branch of psychotherapy called logotherapy, which does not play into the usual ways that people often look at the problems related to the mind and body. It does not simply look at the personality as the ego versus the id or super ego; rather, it recognizes that humankind has a higher calling. It looks closer at whether or not people have meaning in their lives. It ultimately understands that life involves drawing out people's humanity so that they can give themselves more in the service of the beloved. Logotherapy does not simply view life as a mechanical expression in which people try to accumulate or experience as much as possible. It seeks to find a sense of meaning, which of course is quite spiritual. This type of thinking has emerged from studies of cultural mindsets that led to devastating types of genocide and claimed many lives. Such periods of genocide occurred at various times in history such as during the African slave trade, the annihilation of the Native Americans, and during the massive annihilation of the Jewish community.

Dr. Viktor E. Frankl, a top psychiatrist who came up with

this theory was a prisoner in the Jewish concentration camps in Germany during World War II.[5] He noticed that he could practically determine the point at which certain people lost their desire to live. They would start passing stool and urine on themselves without changing and lose all their desire to eat any food. The other prisoners would even know a few days ahead of time that such a person would soon die. He realized that all the people in that environment were experiencing the same types of torture and abuse; however, some people died fast, some people died slowly, and some people did not die at all.

He paid particular attention to those in the environment who underwent the same devastating experiences as other inmates but went on in spite of the suffering. He noticed that the people who had a sense of meaning in their lives and a purpose to go on based on their mental framework lived longer because the consciousness affected the actual body. Some people had a reason to live but when they found their husband or children dead, they also soon lost their own desire to live and died within a few days. Some people lived on because of their own intense belief in God. Other people completely gave up on the idea of God because they could not understand how a God could create such an agonizing situation. Those people would die much faster.

Meaning is a very important conception, and if we lack gratitude, it is harder to develop significant meaning in our lives. We will feel that we do not deserve some of the seemingly negative circumstances in our lives; consequently, we will feel angry and disturbed. We will begin to wonder why God allowed such situations to unfold and why He singled us out instead of someone else. If we lack a healthy sense of meaning about life, that mentality will literally bring on physical death and even spiritual death because a person cannot be a mature spiritualist or spiritual warrior and have weak faith. It does not mean that we should function on blind faith, but it means observing and honoring the Lord's intervention and arrangements. Faith means that we see and act through the eyes of the scripture, and see and act through the lives of the great saints. Many scriptures describe the biographies of these great saints, and we can use such descriptions to make proper evaluations instead of solely relying on our own intelligence and mind.

Remove Yourself from the Center

Most importantly, we do not want to make all of our evaluations with ourselves in the center. It will naturally create problems for us if we make judgments of right or wrong with ourselves at the focal point. We will end up as spiritual failures because the more we place ourselves in the center, the less we will be able to recognize Mother-Father God as the true center. Conversely, the more that we become the servant of the servant, the more we move ourselves away from the center and really become genuinely spiritual. And the more we access genuine spirituality, the more we will remove ourselves from the artificial center.

Ironically, as devotees advance in spiritual life, the Lord will actually move them towards the center and glorify them, but in their own consciousness, they must continue to move away from the center. Therefore, wonderful things genuinely happen to them and around them because they have a sense of gratitude and deeply honor the presence of the Lord. They honor His presence to such an extent that they practically become like His puppets. At the highest level, a conditioned soul can act as a *saktyavesa-avatara* or an empowered living entity who serves as an incarnation of the Lord. They have moved so far from the center that the real center or God actually enters into them in a dominant way and uses them. At this point, whatever they say, do, or think depends on the way God guides them. Again, it depends on the extent to which a person imbibes this sense of gratitude as well as mindfulness. Without sufficient mindfulness and a strong, positive internal dialogue, we will find it difficult to access gratitude.

The Importance of Forgiveness

People often have difficulties with gratitude because they cannot forgive. Since they keep themselves too exclusively in the center, they will repeatedly reflect on the way another person spoke or acted towards them and consequently feel that pain over and over again. However, those who deeply honor the existence of others not only forgive, but they even sometimes place the responsibility on themselves. They consider that their own actions have caused the other person to respond in a negative way; therefore, they apologize to the other person for their own insufficiencies. Not only do they relinquish all grudges, but they also find themselves to be at fault or focus on their own improvements.

Advanced devotees have this mentality. Since they have moved far away from the center and have placed the Lord there instead, when a situation seemingly opposes them, they use it for growth. They even take responsibility by acknowledging that their actions in a previous lifetime may have caused the negative interaction or situation. For example, one Indian gentleman who was extremely offensive would go on walks with Srila Prabhupada, one of my spiritual mentors, and have discussions with him. At one point, Srila Prabhupada said that he must have done something to the man in a previous lifetime, emphasizing through his humility that one does not honor the duality.

The *Bhagavad-gita* says that a *sadhu* or saint does not become the enemy of his or her enemy, which means that even if someone steps forward to act as an enemy, a *sadhu* does not accept that position in return. The purport to texts 14.22-25 of the *Bhagavad-gita* explains:

> He [the transcendentally situated person] takes everyone as his dear friend who helps him in his execution of Krishna consciousness, and he does not hate his so-called enemy. He is equally disposed and sees everything on an equal level because he knows perfectly well that he has nothing to do with material existence.

Once we accept a person as our enemy, it means that we must now try to destroy him or her; consequently, we become like that person. But as we honor the presence of God and remove ourselves from the center, then we do not feel attacked and we do not have to respond in such a negative way either. We can continue absorbing ourselves in love and devotion while glorifying the Lord instead of allowing such distractions to capture us. Without sufficient mindfulness; a strong, positive internal dialogue; gratitude; a sense of forgiveness; and the attentive observance and eradication of the enemies of the mind, a person will surely become distracted and the mind will become the greatest enemy.

Seeing the Extraordinary in the Ordinary

Sometimes we also find it difficult to feel grateful because once the novelty of an experience wears off, we settle into patterns and then the mundaneness sets in. However, if we understand how the residents of the spiritual world think and live, we can gradually develop those qualities by imbibing that same nature. In the spiritual world, every meeting and interaction is a fresh exchange. We can carry a greater sense of gratitude into our relationships if we can also treat every interaction like a first meeting, a first chance to serve, a first chance to appreciate, or a first chance to associate with that other person. By maintaining this mentality, we will not begin to take each other or the other aspects of the devotional culture for granted. If we see every exchange as new and fresh, we will feel much more ecstatic as each experience unfolds. We can improve the quality of our spiritual relationships in this way. When we gather to take *darsana*, read together, or engage in *bhajana* or singing as a group, we can appreciate the association more by reflecting on it as new and fresh. We do not just want to make any type of impression or good first impressions, but we want to relate in a joyful, compassionate, comprehensive fresh mood during each encounter that we have with others.

After we accustom ourselves to certain patterns, we will begin to accept them as ordinary. The *arati* or religious service, the *Bhagavad-gita* class, or the *kirtana* will begin to seem like any other ordinary activity. We will also start to see our associates as ordinary, considering that the person is just my wife, my son, my husband, my daughter, my spiritual director, or my godbrother. We will minimize their ultimate identity as eternal spiritual entities connected with the Supreme Lord. This type of mentality distinctly indicates that we lack gratitude. When we think in this way, we will become cynical or critical while minimizing those things that can free us of these diseases. By maintaining this mindset, we will block off the potency of powerful spiritual practices or associations.

If we engage in a transcendental activity, we will definitely gain some benefit. However, we also benefit according to our level of knowledge, understanding, and submission. The same potent experience or activity affects two or three people in very different ways. One person may have the experience, but if he or she does not have the knowledge or a submissive attitude, he or she will not receive the full benefit. The more we have potent experiences while simultaneously understanding the purpose, the more it will affect and benefit our well-being and consciousness. If we lack the proper understanding and receptivity, we will still benefit but not to the same degree.

By maintaining a mood of appreciation and surrender, all our engagements will have more of an effect. The more we pray, meditate, and chant with understanding, the more powerful of an effect it will have. As we call on the names of God, we can reflect on the Lord's names as non-different from Himself. The holy name is our eternal fax line to the spiritual kingdom and the connection that we can have with eternal spiritual beings. Even *caranamrta* or sacred water and *prasadam* will not affect each individual in the same way. It depends on the element of consciousness and on the level of reverence and appreciation for the spiritualized water or foodstuff. This endeavor to rise above the unhealthy dualities of the three modes of material nature is what really binds us together as spiritual warriors.

Attitude is Crucial

We are addressing this subject matter in order to draw more attention to the importance of attitude. Our spiritual lives revolve around service and relationships, but attitude is even more important than just the external service we render. We engage in the physical in order to develop more of the internal service attitude. If the practitioner lacks the proper attitude, he or she will achieve minimal results. Although we may do so much, know so much, and arrange so much, the Lord looks at the attitude. It is the devotional attitude or consciousness that really penetrates the modes of material nature and all mundane duality.

When we do not have the proper mentality, we can even act mechanically lifetime after lifetime without getting the results. Even in terms of the holy name, we can chant and pray for many lifetimes, but if we chant offensively we will still not achieve the results or come to the Vasudeva platform or the platform of seeing God face-to-face. We can perform so many sacrifices and rituals but still not accelerate the purity of the spirituality if we simply act out of a desire to acquire something from the Lord. We will simply end up engaging in *karma-misra-bhakti*, *yoga-misra-bhakti*, and *jnana-misra-bhakti*. Although the *bhakti* or devotion is included in these endeavors, it gets contaminated by *jnana* or an interest in knowledge; by *yoga* or an interest in mystic *siddhis*; or by *karma* or an interest in fruitive results. Consequently, the person's concerns simply revolve around their own desires. They mainly care about what they will get from the Lord and what they will experience from the *sakti* or energy rather than what they can offer to the *sakti-man* or energetic. The person will even associate with others in order to enhance their own personal plan.

Unfortunately, when we come with this kind of mixed mood, the Lord helps us by giving us some hard love. In other words, He will find ways to show us our shortcomings with the hope that we will change. However, it can still take some people a long time if they refuse to see their weaknesses. When people have either an inferiority complex or an inflated ego, even though the Lord might send them so much to help them see or understand, they will not really properly accept it. It can take a long time for them to process the help. It might even take a serious disaster in a person's life such as a death or some other sort of calamity to help them wake up. Some people will only make a big shift in their consciousness when a calamity hits, which they might need in order to shake them out of their illusion. Then they will begin to look closer at their own lives and begin to develop more gratitude. It is unfortunate when it has to come in this way because the person wastes so much time and undergoes so much pain before he or she finally accepts the actual realities.

Blessed by the Best

Many years ago, before they both passed due to cancer, my mother and aunt came to visit us at the Institute for Applied Spiritual Technology, which I founded in Washington, D.C. My aunt had an amazing way of responding to people. She had a very difficult situation because she had many children and grandchildren, was a widow, and had problems throughout the family. However, whenever you called her or asked, "How are you?" she recited this *mantra*, "I am blessed by the best." In spite of all of these other economic, social, or family difficulties, she constantly thanked the Lord and she always had this type of vibrancy.

Actually, the only disability is attitude. Therapists sometimes present this maxim to individuals who have handicaps because such disabilities do not interfere with a person's ability to love, serve, or thank God. Unfortunately, some people with disabilities just remain morbid and dismal, and they lose the chance to grow and excel within their situation. Or they simply wait for other people to do what they should be able to do for themselves. Consequently, they go year after year totally frustrated and depressed. Such people do not have a deep level of spirituality because a spiritualist will understand the influence of *karma* in their lives but still find ways to honor the Lord and appreciate others.

However, both a large false ego and a lack of self-esteem minimize God. As we have stressed, low self-esteem is actually another way of playing God. We play God by focusing so much on ourselves that we end up only thinking about ourselves. We just think about the money, the relationship, the love, or the health that we do not have. It is all about our body, our concerns, our needs, and our disappointments, and then we even begin to feel angry that such needs have not been satisfied. We basically lack gratitude. However, we must realize that the only disability is our attitude because so much of our material and spiritual situation depends on attitude.

The Lord responds to us according to our quality of surrender, and if we take that a step further, we see that surrender often relates to consciousness. It does not entirely depend on secondary considerations such as what we give and what we avoid; it depends more on the consciousness behind those actions. Every aspect of the devotional culture such as the rituals, scriptures, associations, and paraphernalia are all designed to stimulate our internal consciousness. If these stimuli only remain external, then a person has cheated him or herself and has minimized the mercy that the Lord and His great servants constantly provide. It never has been and never will be about the individual in the center or about external factors.

A Lesson in Every Situation

While reflecting on some of the amazing projects and teaching activities throughout the world in which I assist, I feel grateful for the Lord's kindness because many of these unusual events are taking place in spite of us. I feel grateful to see that many spiritual warriors, devotees, and disciples in many places around the world are growing, but I also see that some devotees are not growing so well due to their minds. However, this type of stagnation is also beneficial because people learn from every situation. Sometimes we learn the easy way but sometimes we learn through tough love or various other difficulties. Nevertheless, learning takes place. As long as we engage in activity, have blessings from the present and ascended masters, and avoid offenses, all of our circumstances will form a part of the growth experience.

Vaisnava-aparadha, or offenses against the devotees of the Lord, are the main factors that will cause us to move backwards instead of forwards. Unfortunately, *vaisnava-aparadha* eventually leads to *guru-aparadha* and then to blasphemy of God Himself. That can happen and will happen because as the confusion from the sinful culture accelerates, people's minds will go one way or the other. People will either develop an awareness of how to grow along with a greater sense of spiritual gratitude or they will simply begin to focus on what they lack in their lives. Of course, if they focus on the negative, it will increase the stagnation rather than the growth.

In one sense, when we develop gratitude, we increase our appreciation of the positive aspects of our lives, and give less attention to the seemingly negative aspects. Proper gratitude means that we always have faith in the Lord as our well-wisher and always honor the indwelling presence of the Lord as *para-*

matma. We will eagerly want to honor that presence of the Divinity within every person.

> *sarvasya caham hrdi sannivisto*
> *mattah smrtir jnanam apohanam ca*
>
> I am seated in everyone's heart, and from Me come remembrance, knowledge and forgetfulness.
> *Bhagavad-gita* 15.15

If we really recognize God's presence everywhere, how can we not have a strong sense of gratitude? How can we not develop gratitude if we really understand that God's mercy is greater than His law? How can we not develop gratitude if we recognize that every moment is a chance to try to love the Lord and other people more, and actually strategize to increase the quality of our service? How can we not develop gratitude after recognizing the fact that this very body in this lifetime is an opportunity to free ourselves once and for all of birth, old age, disease, and death? How can we not have gratitude if we remind ourselves that the Lord is always so close, residing in our hearts, monitoring us, and waiting to be fully discovered in order to shower us with loving ecstasy?

We have the opportunity in this very lifetime to do the necessary so that we will never again have to deal with any types of duality or suffering. If we reflect on all these amazing truths, we will naturally develop extreme gratitude. However, we will definitely have problems if we just think very selfishly because we will remain captured by lust and self-centeredness. We will simply end up looking at what we want and how we can reach that end while disregarding *sadhu*, *sastra*, and *guru* or saints, scriptures, and the spiritual master. Without gratitude, we will only see the stagnations and feel that our material situation should manifest much faster. Try my aunt's *mantra* for a few days or why not make it a part of your salutation. It will help you and others to think more of God's mercy.

Hearing from the Scriptures

There are many stories in the Vaisnava tradition as well as in other theologies that emphasize the importance of a proper attitude, which will lead to auspiciousness and spiritual progression. For example, the *Caitanya-bhagavata, Madhya-khanda*, Chapter 23, in the Vaisnava tradition, describes the wonderful *kirtanas* that went on in Srivasa Thakura's house. Lord Caitanya and His wonderful associates would come together to participate in nighttime *kirtanas* and associate with those who had a similar mentality. Such devotees were completely surrendered, completely in love with the Lord, and completely aware of Krishna's position as the supreme controller. Since they understood the supreme position of the Lord, they could also understand that there are no accidents. Therefore, they had the highest expression of gratitude and could properly glorify the Lord while associating with one another.

Once a young *brahmacari* who wanted to come and participate in the environment approached Srivasa Thakura. He was extremely austere and very knowledgeable. He took an austere *vrata* or vow that he would just drink a little milk, remaining oblivious to the material body and material world because he desperately desired to get the mercy of the Lord. Some austerities are so intense that they say "death to the physical" and "life to the eternal" or the spirit. In other words, by denying the physical, sometimes a person has really taken some serious steps to try to avoid the duality. It means that the person puts him or herself in a completely dependent position on the Lord. Rigorous austerities have that kind of background connection. Such practices really say, "I completely belong to You, Lord. Do with me as You like. I am ready to move so far away from the center that I am no longer even concerned about eating, living conditions, fame, adoration, or distinction. I am taking myself fully out of the center so that I can honor You and worship You intensely."

This *brahmacari* or celibate student had this type of mentality because he had minimized the things that people normally pursue for themselves. Consequently, Srivasa Thakura felt that he was a very special person and eagerly wanted to invite him into their association. During the *kirtana*, Lord Caitanya noticed a difference in the atmosphere and in the ecstasy because whatever we carry spills over into the environment. He could understand that some visitor had been invited. He later distinctly asked about the visitor and Srivasa made it clear that he had in fact invited this *brahmacari*. Although Srivasa Thakura described his austerities and other achievements, such descriptions did not impress Lord Caitanya. Sri Caitanya Mahaprabhu explained that austerities alone cannot get His mercy, even these very extreme levels of commitment or austerities. Although knowledge, rituals, and austerities function as prerequisites, they cannot really purchase the Lord. Krishna may easily give *mukti* (liberation), *bhukti* (material enjoyment), and *siddhi* (mystic perfections), but He will not give *bhakti* quite as easily. A person must first become a *bhakta* and give himself fully in order to receive the Lord.

Lord Caitanya then chastised Srivasa and ordered the *brahmacari* to leave. However, although the *brahmacari* had to relinquish that association, he felt so grateful for the few moments in that extraordinary environment. He departed with this extreme mood of gratitude, deeply appreciating that brief chance to absorb himself in that atmosphere. However, as he left, Lord Caitanya could understand his mood of gratitude. Although the boy's powerful austerities did not impress Him, his appreciation and gratitude actually caught Lord Caitanya's attention. Consequently, Lord Caitanya called him back and allowed him to take part in the ongoing exchanges.

Sridhara Kholaveca, during this same time period, also exemplifies this mood. *Sri Caitanya-caritamrta* describes how he did not have much money and simply sold cups and plates made from banana leaves to earn his livelihood. However, in spite of his seemingly abject position, he was so ecstatic, eager, and grateful. He would use fifty percent of the little money that he earned from his sales for service and *puja* although he could barely maintain himself. Nevertheless, he felt so grateful for the opportunity to even use the little money that he had in the Lord's service. Lord Caitanya Himself came to see him regularly and even wanted some of his wares. At one point during one of their exchanges, Caitanya Mahaprabhu embraced him and caused him to experience the highest level of love due to this attitude. Sridhara did not look at his material deficiencies or envy the possessions of other people; he simply appreciated that which came his way and offered it all back to the Lord.

The Nectar of Devotion explains a concept called *daya-bhak*, which refers to the idea that a devotee should continue serving Krishna with perseverance in spite of the many difficulties. It says in the *Srimad-Bhagavatam* 10.14.8:

> My dear Lord, one who earnestly waits for You to bestow Your causeless

mercy upon him, all the while patiently suffering the reactions of his past misdeeds and offering You respectful obeisances with his heart, words and body, is surely eligible for liberation, for it has become his rightful claim.

Although we may have committed many sinful activities and must continue to receive the reactions, we should maintain a certain level of consciousness as well as gratitude because in time it will become our rightful claim to return to the Kingdom of God.

Srila Sridhara Swami explains in his commentary that just as a legitimate son has to simply remain alive to gain an inheritance from his father, one who simply remains alive in Krishna consciousness, following the regulative principles of *bhakti-yoga,* automatically becomes eligible to receive the mercy of the Personality of Godhead. In other words, he will be promoted to the Kingdom of God.
Srimad-Bhagavatam 10.14.8, purport

However, we must carefully maintain our spiritual life through gratitude and by accessing the science in a proper way. If we lose our enthusiasm along with our entire spiritual life, we will not inherit this wealth. We will then allow obstacles to disturb us although they could have been valuable opportunities. If we serve mechanically or allow our egos to take over, we will also lose our spiritual life. Somehow, we simply have to go on in order to inherit the wonderful assets.

Access Gratitude in Your Own Lives

We call on you to start accessing more gratitude in your lives. You can start by thinking of yourselves less and more of others. You can also increase your gratitude by appreciating the events in your past and looking towards the future. When you do feel angry or allow the enemies of the mind to come forth, you can then immediately drag the mind back to the positive aspects of your life. Consequently, you will draw more of Mother-Father God's mercy because you will have properly reposed your attitude in the right place.

We want to look closer at this subject so that all of you can accelerate more in your spiritual lives. Spiritual life is a simple science but due to its simplicity, it sometimes seems complex. It does not depend on how many books we read, how many *yajnas* we perform, or how many years we have been chanting, meditating, or praying. It does not even depend on where we go, how we dress, or what we do. It mostly depends on how we think. The physical body is temporary which means that our consciousness is more deeply connected with our real existence. It is the consciousness at the time of death that determines where the soul goes. The destination of the soul does not in any way depend on the amount of money in our bank account, the type of house we own, the quantity of *yajnas* we perform, or our associates; it depends on our consciousness and attitude. We must transform the mind from our greatest enemy into our greatest friend. Arise spiritual warriors—for this is our life's work!

Questions and Answers

Question: How do we appreciate the spiritual master more on a subtle level? We often appreciate the *guru* more when he personally gives us a certain service or gives us instructions. However, when we pray to the spiritual master in his physical absence, we understand that we have a connection and that he gives us blessings. For instance, before we begin a service, we may pray to the spiritual master for his mercy in order to properly carry it out, but because some of us are so analytical, we may only recognize things by actually physically seeing them. How does this process of praying for strength and empowerment work when we so often have to serve in the spiritual master's physical absence?

Answer: Again, it is so simple but also complex. It is all about God. Many living entities have turned their backs on the Lord but some want to turn toward Him. As we turn towards the Lord, He arranges various interactions. One of these interactions involves spiritual mentorship. The spiritual mentor actually acts as a coach to remind us that God is personal and that treasures are waiting for us as we move ourselves away from the center. Krishna is in the heart and is speaking to everyone. He is bringing us back to His love but we are imposing the obstacles. The obstacles appear when we minimize *sadhu*, *sastra*, and *guru*, or they may manifest when we do not receive the proper purports from *sastra*, the proper appreciation from *sadhu*, or the proper help and guidance from *guru*.

As we think of ourselves less and think more of the Supreme Personality of Godhead and other people, we will naturally connect with everyone on a deeper level. And it definitely means that we will connect more deeply with the *guru* because

An Attitude of Gratitude

he is a catalyst for God. If we try to come more genuinely to the Supreme in the proper attitude, not only will the spiritual master become a more distinct part of our consciousness and try to help us, we will gradually begin to see that the bona fide *guru* is not just an isolated personality; he is a particular type of servant and ambassador of God. However, when we remain locked in our own mindset, we will see the world from our perspective and categorize things accordingly.

Question: Your Holiness, can you share more about how low self-esteem acts as an enemy to our spiritual progress?

Answer: Some people have such an inferiority complex that they will not be able to see certain things. Someone might speak nicely to them or give them gifts but they may not respond due to their own feelings of unworthiness. They cannot really accept that it came to them or that the other person meant to honor them because they do not feel worthy of honor or appreciation. On the other hand, a person might have such a large false ego that they simply cannot tune into the blessings in their lives because the ego clouds their consciousness with so many other distractions. Realization in spiritual life actually depends on what we become free of rather than what we gain because we are already fully pure in our original nature. However, due to our acculturation, which has interfered with that purity, we must now try to participate in the spiritual activities in order to free ourselves of these blocks. Once we become free of the blocks, our natural, vibrant spiritual self will come forth.

The great *sadhus* do not have any inferiority complexes or a lack of self-esteem due to their humility; they just have so much esteem for Krishna and for others. It is not quite the same. Modern day psychology immediately categorizes humility as low self-esteem. However, spiritual life is not about low self-esteem; rather, it is about high esteem and high gratitude for God and for all things associated with Him. The more a devotee develops purity, the less he or she will interfere with the Lord's plan. It is just that simple. Through deep analysis and appreciation, we will see that the Lord has arranged everything for us. For instance, if you really love someone, you will go out of your way to arrange exactly what he or she likes. You may cook for her or offer all types of services, but the individual ultimately has to come forward in order to accept.

Similarly, Krishna or God has made all the arrangements according to the desires of every living entity. Someone might want to love the Lord as a beautiful child; therefore, Krishna arranges to have someone love Him fully in that relationship. Someone else has the desire for a deep friendship so Krishna arranges that the person can have the most wonderful friendship ever imaginable. If a person wants to reciprocate in the mood of a servant, Krishna creates the perfect servant-master arrangement.

Not only does He create the perfect relationship according to each living entity's wishes, but the environment also perfectly corresponds to these different types of relationships. If someone wants the Lord as a lover, He then arranges the perfect atmosphere. Then the lover and beloved can reciprocate with the most opulent paraphernalia. Just as lovers in the material world dress nicely, want to hear beautiful music, and go to nice places together, the Lord arranges all of that better than any expert architect or designer. We simply have to accept His arrangements. However, this material world is filled with living entities who have temporarily turned their backs on the Lord's expert arrangements, but He is gradually finding ways to return us to His dynamic abode. Our low self-esteem makes us feel that we are not worthy of God's arrangements, care, and love. Such an internal dialogue shuts the Lord out and denies His mercy.

Question: Sometimes we find that some elevated spiritual personalities have differences in their opinions. Some people may even become critical as a result. For instance, many great *acaryas* were very revolutionary, but those who could not appreciate their behavior and vision would categorize their actions as improper. How can we appreciate the different aspects of the philosophy presented by these various personalities, which might seemingly contradict the opinions of other personalities, especially the more conservative?

Answer: Higher personalities act as puppets in the Lord's hands, which means that they will do whatever will please the Supreme. If God wants to use a puppet to spread the *yuga-dharma* or current, relevant religious practices to a certain part of the world, then that puppet will allow him or herself to be used in that specific orientation. If He wants to use the puppet to preach to a certain class of people, then the puppet will also function accordingly. Since every great *acarya* fully places him or herself at God's service, they all have unique differences. We can understand that their similarities result from their full surrender to the Lord. They have similarities since they do not embrace sense gratification, and they use every moment and situation to glorify the Lord.

In material life, we determine status through external designations such as a person's salary, the neighborhood in which they reside, or the car that they drive, but if we bring these factors into spiritual life, we will simply fall victim to the same type of material categories. Consequently, we may end up focusing too much on these external factors that are in fact material. However, by reading more closely the biographies of these great personalities, we will see great unity with diversity and we will also understand what type of arrangements can change and what cannot change. We need to clearly understand the difference between the details and the essence. We will see that these great personalities make all types of arrangements to get the essence through because they are madly in love with the Lord and are being used by Him very directly. It is all about consciousness, which is connected to selfless love and service.

The differences between very highly elevated personalities may stem from their eternal connection with the Lord. Due to their particular, eternal service to the Lord, they may place their emphasis in a certain area that the materialist or neophyte simply cannot understand. Furthermore, sometimes very evolved beings have a unique commission, which is the meaning of *acarya*. According to their commission, they have a certain format that they follow. Spiritual life is not a monotonous affair but an exciting adventure. It is not dry or just a matter of rituals and ceremonies. It is full of loving adventures of the soul. All the other concerns are in the background and a part of the stage for the actual dynamic spiritual unions and connections.

Question: Can you elaborate on the basic obstacles that can prevent a person from developing a good attitude?

Answer: The obstacles develop when we do not accept the Supreme Lord as our well-wisher. Consequently, we will not look at the events in our lives with a sense of appreciation. We have the choice to look at what we lack or to look at what we have. If we have a greater sense of appreciation, the Supreme then makes the next arrangement. We should try to constantly think, "How can I serve the Lord?" We want to always remember the Lord and never forget Him, and accept all things that are favorable to devotional service and reject all things that are unfavorable. Then we have to find out what is favorable. We can ask ourselves, "Does this activity help me to honor *sadhus* better? Will this help me situate myself more at the mercy of my *guru's* order and service? Will this help me think of myself less and think more of others? Will this help me become a better servant?" On the other hand, we might need to ask, "Is this causing me to feel that I deserve or need more?"

We have all seen people who have a genuine handicap, but they do not accept the handicap. Although the slightest activities challenge them, they do for themselves and eagerly speak positively whenever you talk to them. They are happy about life and are pleasant to be around. However, in other cases, you may not want to be around some people who have handicaps because they simply drain you. Some people may not even have such an issue but due to their lack of gratitude, you just find it hard to spend time with them. For instance, they might want a new car even though they already drive a fairly new one or they might want a ten million dollar house although they already live in a three million dollar home. An athlete might feel so angry that he won the silver instead of the gold in the Olympics. He simply feels miserable because of what he did not do. Another person might have wanted to corner the stock market in a certain way but someone else got the leverage over them. Due to their fury, they practically want to commit suicide.

It could help us to visit some of the villages in which people have been living quite simply generation after generation. It might shock you to see that the people have a sense of happiness. They use what they have and work with a sense of community. The individuals tend to support one another, which helps them feel good about themselves. Although they have so little, some do not feel any type of want. However, when those same people have to deal with what they do not have, they might then lose their peace. If some intrusion or acculturation begins to break down their way of life, sometimes the people will begin to hoard and gradually lose their natural simplicity and appreciation.

We can engage in all types of worship, but if we do not have a service mentality or recognize *guru* and Krishna's constant presence, we will not have much potency. Then, when we interact in society, the various distractions will simply agitate and drain us. However, if we consider ourselves to be on a mission for the Lord, the distractions will not affect us so intensely. To the degree that we think of ourselves as the experiencers, we will want to experience and constantly endeavor to maximize our selfish pleasure. However, to the degree that we position ourselves as puppets for the Lord, the enticements will not disturb us.

Once we try to experience on our own or begin to maximize our experiences, thoughts, and feelings, we will have problems. The body will naturally have some attraction to certain objects because the body and mind function in this way. It is natural for a boy to be attracted to a girl and for a girl to be attracted to a boy. It is natural for the mind to be attracted to all types of subtle allurements. Furthermore, to the degree that we identify with our physical body and the bodies of other people, the enticements will continue to lure us in. By moving ourselves out of the center and by viewing our service as part of the mission of the *guru* and the Lord, we can move around in a mood of detachment. Then, when an allurement directly comes before us and invites us for sense gratification, we will not feel disturbed because we are not serving for our own gratification. We are not out there to experience or enjoy, but we are to make arrangements as the Lord's puppets.

These are simple concepts but quite profound. We just have to take the science more seriously and move out of the way. The more that we are in the way, the more we will have to deal with obstacles based on our personality and desires. Haridasa Thakura, a very pure saint in the Vaisnava tradition, is a nice example. A prostitute came to lure him away from his *bhajana* or worship, but he did not think in terms of the body by trying to enjoy. On the other hand, he did not feel repulsed by her or try to get rid of her through some violent attack. He did not think, "I am a saint. Why are you bothering me?" He ultimately thought of himself as a servant of God and also saw her from this same perspective. He saw her as a servant of the Lord who had just forgotten her position and he understood that they both belong to the Supreme. Due to this vision, he had the strength to dodge the attack of *maya* and instead transform the *maya* by purifying her and by elevating her consciousness.

It actually takes a sufficient amount of energy to go for the sense gratification and fall prey to it. It also takes energy to fight against the attacks. However, if we just constantly try to fight, we might even create the very situation that we most want to avoid due to our constant meditation on the allurement. We do not want to get caught up in too much fighting or avoidance. We honor the allurement but we honor it in a higher way. It is natural that we will feel attracted to the things that our culture labels as beautiful or exciting. It varies according to people, culture, heredity, and environment but when such stimuli are present and we are identifying with them, we will want to enjoy. However, we want to be in the world but not of the world. The body and mind will naturally try to connect with sense gratification but we can try to honor the stimuli as beautiful while appreciating it as an aspect of the Lord's energy.

At the end of one of the workshops I gave in Ireland many years ago, one of the ladies who is a medical doctor and also attractive concluded the program by dancing a very special cultural dance called Bharata Natyam. Although people's minds will definitely view the dance in different ways, we can perceive the performance as a wonderful expression of culture and devotion while seeing every gesture as an offering to God. These dancers must receive special training in order to engage in this very intense spiritual dance. For instance, in India, some performers even receive this training from birth in order to dance for Lord Jagannatha. Only certain families and people enact the special pastimes, which go on in Vrndavana, through dance because they must have a sufficient level of purity. Since they are representing the spiritual connection, one should not be mundanely attracted to these performers.

However, the mind can go in many directions. On one hand, the mind might think, "She dances so nicely. She should be mine. Her performance is just for me." The mind can also think, "What a wonderful expression of Krishna consciousness." Although people view the same performance, everyone will perceive it differently according to their consciousness. But if one identifies too mundanely with that situation, the senses can become disturbed.

We want to genuinely appreciate the dance because, in the spiritual world, so many expert performances constantly unfold in the most expert ways. When the spiritual entities dance in the spiritual world, they dance greater than anyone else could ever dance in this realm. When they sing, they sing better than anyone else. Even their cooking or dressing far excels any material attempt. We will find so much powerful opulence in the spiritual world because everything is at its highest level of perfection. A difference between the material world and the spiritual world is that in this realm people do not perform so well and even when there are high achievements, the suffering is still present. The spiritual world is so full of activities but the pure devotees engage in every activity for Krishna.

One swami once addressed a similar topic in a class while speaking to some devotees who were having trouble with opulence. He pointed out that the spiritual world is very opulent. Vaikuntha is very opulent but Krishnaloka is very opulent in another way. Everything is beautiful and perfectly arranged. However, in spite of this opulence, people do not have the desire to own it for themselves. The problems arise when we try to own Krishna's opulence for our own pleasure. However, in spiritual life, the more you give up, ironically the more God gives you until He gives you everything. He gives you everything according to your ultimate relationship with Him and gives everything that makes that relationship sweet.

We have a choice. Do we continue to endeavor for these temporary relationships and connections or do we pay the price in this lifetime so that we can eternally connect with the perfect relationships and experiences? We can make this decision ourselves. We can try to enjoy on our own in this material body, which we really cannot fully do in the first place, or we can gradually try to offer everything back to God so that we can once again have all these experiences with Him. Each person makes a choice.

Question: Can you explain how this same understanding relates to children? As they go in and out of different associations and experience their natural desires, how can we as parents assist our children?

Answer: First of all, we can go back through our own memory and remind ourselves of our own experiences as children. By reflecting on some of the desires that we had, some of the secrets we kept, things that made us happy, or some things that we took as impositions, we will understand how complex it is for a child. We should then take all of our memories and multiply them several times because children must now face so many more confrontations. We grew up in a time when people still had a little truth and faith left. Now, whether it involves institutions, leadership, or even the president, the big lies are the most intriguing aspects of this time period. Such lies might involve the conspiracy behind JFK and Dr. Martin Luther King Jr.; the deviations of the FBI or CIA; the disposal of toxic waste; nuclear, biological, and chemical weapons; or extraterrestrials. On top of so many lies, they must also deal with virtual reality because photography, media, or even print can produce so many ideas and even propaganda that can make a concocted idea seem real.

Children will naturally find it difficult to know what to embrace when their education, recreation, and social life involve cosmetic and relative arrangements. Enjoyment is relative and even the genders can be relative. Their philosophy, ethics, or science classes now explain to them that these issues differ from what we originally thought. They see all of this on television, in books, and from many other sources. Then, spiritualists often try to present them with some autocratic or universal standards in the midst of all of these other relative considerations. As a parent, it is quite difficult to deal with your children in the presence of all these factors. Furthermore, many times the peer pressure outweighs the parental pressure unless other adults can also provide support. You just have to do your best and pray.

Question: My brother came to my home recently with all of his opulences such as a new car and other material possessions. When he saw me in my small apartment, he felt so anxious and miserable, wondering how I could feel so happy. He has all types of opportunities to facilitate him and I have nothing materially equivalent but I am very happy due to my spirituality.

Answer: We can all understand this feeling just by looking at our own lives. If we examine the times when we felt the happiest, we will understand that it does not always depend on the physical scheme; rather, it depends on our consciousness. In some of the Western countries and especially in America, we can have an even greater awareness of this fact. In many places where people do not have so many material possessions, they might find this concept more difficult to understand because they see other people with so much opulence and then they hanker to have it as well. When people do not have a car or house, and they have to live in a place with fifteen or more other people, they will endlessly desire a house of their own.

We live in America, a part of the world in which people have basic material possessions. Even the average person who some might consider poor will have many basic material items. In many other parts of the world, that same person would be considered upper-middle class. In some countries, just owning a car categorizes a person as upper-middle class. Here, in America, even a person working for minimum wage or receiving welfare can have one or two cars and live at a fairly high standard.

A certain type of consciousness produces a serial killer or a child abuser. A certain type of consciousness leads to racism, tribalism, homicide, or suicide. Everything starts and ends with consciousness. A certain type of consciousness allows a person to reside in hellish environments and remain happy. However, another person can attain heavenly surroundings but mentally reside in hell. Actually, the happiest person in spiritual life is one who has relinquished all personal desires for happiness and simply wants to act as a selfless, pure servant. Such a person who has moved him or herself out of the center will have the highest level of realization and happiness. On the other hand, the person who constantly tries to remain the controller will advance slowly and will experience the most duality and frustration. Such a person will constantly be defeated by the enemies of the mind.

We cannot simultaneously embrace the spiritual path and engage in *maya* while still hoping to develop Krishna consciousness. Every time we say yes to *maya*, we turn our backs on Krishna. Every time we say no to *maya*, we begin to move closer towards Krishna's loving embrace. Life involves acceleration. As we grow older, we should also grow in wisdom and increase our hunger for spiritual life as the challenges accelerate. Such an attitude is associated with **healthy gratitude**. Remember to remind yourself and others that you are **blessed by the best and will not settle for anything less!**

Chapter 4

The Necessity of Enthusiasm

*viraktas cendriya-ratau
bhakti-yogena bhuyasa
tam nirantara-bhavena
bhajetaddha vimuktaye*

If one is very serious about liberation, he must stick to the process of transcendental loving service, engaging twenty-four hours a day in the highest stage of ecstasy, and he must certainly be aloof from all activities of sense gratification.
Srimad-Bhagavatam 4.8.61

Enthusiasm Leads to Success

In the process of examining the enemies of the mind, we must find out how they attack and how to recover from the attacks when they do happen. Most importantly, we want to know how to avoid the attacks before they take place. *Utsaha* or enthusiasm plays a significant role in protecting ourselves as well as removing the obstacles that interfere with our minds in the process of devotional service. We want to scrutinize this topic from all angles so that we can understand what produces enthusiasm, what hinders its development, what happens in its presence, and what happens in its absence.

If we look at spiritual success and even secular success, we will see a connection between enthusiasm, patience, conviction, and determination. Such qualities are of course spiritual. Conversely, if we look at failure—spiritual or secular—we will see a constant manifestation of a lack of enthusiasm. Great saints and devotees such as Srila Rupa Gosvami list enthusiasm as one of the primary tenets that help us surrender to the Lord. Why does enthusiasm play such an important role? It should be evident, because we all notice the effects of a lack of enthusiasm. The demands of the senses increase and the enemies of the mind, such as *kama* (lust), *krodha* (anger), *lobha* (greed), *moha* (illusion), *matsarya* (enviousness), and *mada* (madness) attack us. Not only do the six enemies devastate us, their close associates such as *mana* (pride), *bhaya* (fear), *soka* (lamentation), and *visada* (depression) also attack. Each of these enemies can infiltrate our minds and engulf our consciousness, particularly when we lack enthusiasm. This should help us understand the power of enthusiasm because it builds our spiritual immune system and provides a unique type of protection. When we are enthusiastic, we are more mindful and grateful, we have more short and long-term goals, and, most important, we have a powerful internal dialogue. In the absence of enthusiasm, we will experience more disturbances because we will not have the potency to dispel attacks.

Our enthusiasm will naturally fluctuate according to the types of experiences we anticipate in the future. If a person finds out that they will receive a million dollars next week, he or she will feel very enthusiastic due to the anticipation of the experience. The individual would probably begin planning ways to use the money even before its actual arrival. On the other hand, how can you feel enthusiastic if you know that in one week, the landlord and the bank plan to evict you from your house since you have not paid your mortgage? Not only will they take your house, but they also plan to repossess your car and send you to jail since you have broken the law. How can you feel enthusiastic? What we anticipate has a major influence on our consciousness. Most people's lives are quite materialistic so they ultimately have little to look forward to other than getting evicted from their bodies and having what they possess taken away. At death, they cannot claim ownership. Reflecting on these cold realities stops a person's enthusiasm.

Misdirected Enthusiasm

Billions of people in the world have misdirected enthusiasm, but millions of them have no enthusiasm at all. Who is in the most difficult situation—those who have misdirected enthusiasm or those who have no enthusiasm? Who suffers the most intensely? Those who have no enthusiasm have no excitement or taste, either material or spiritual. Depression affects approximately 16 million people in the United States and 100 million people worldwide to such an extent that they will require medical treatment at some point in their lives.[6] Furthermore, depression costs employers more money than any other problem in the workplace, amounting to approximately $43.7 billion dollars every year. Such expenses result from lost time due to absenteeism, lack of productivity, depression related suicides, and medical care.[7] Some people suffer from such severe depression that they cannot eat, bathe, or even get out of bed. They basically have no passion or enthusiasm to do anything. They have no enthusiasm for life and no enthusiasm for deviation. In this state, people can hardly attempt to follow spiritual activities.

Actually, everyone ultimately wants to experience *ruci* or taste although most people simply run after *capala-sukha* or flickering and temporary sense enjoyment. Unfortunately, this type of pleasure has long-term negative and inauspicious results. Although it might produce immediate stimulation, it ultimately involves misdirected energy, consciousness, and activities. Many times we feel very enthusiastic when it comes to sense gratification, and we might find ways to access the maximum amount of sense enjoyment, but when it comes to unconditional devotional service, we find it hard to find the excitement.

In order to progress on the spiritual path, we must figure out where we want to direct our enthusiasm. We do not want to increase our enthusiasm for gross or subtle sense gratification nor do we want to be void of any enthusiasm. Not only do some people have no enthusiasm for anything spiritual, but they do not have enthusiasm for even social, political, or financial pursuits. They have no enthusiasm to try to understand God nor do they have any enthusiasm to try to avoid the Lord's service through deviation. We want *utsaha* or enthusiasm, but we want to direct it in the proper way. And we want it continuously because it makes our existence more meaningful and it helps us appreciate the medicine that will lead us to ultimate liberation and service. It will help us check the enemies that are constantly attacking us in the mind and influencing our entire life.

Find Time for Introspection

Take a moment to remember the times on your own spiritual quest when you felt most enthusiastic. We want to pinpoint the times in which we felt more God conscious and devotional than ever before. Conversely, look at the times when you felt unenthused and do a similar analysis. These questions might help stimulate your thought process: Are you enthusiastic about your existence as a servant of the Lord? Are you enthusiastic to follow the basic principles that will help elevate your consciousness? Are you enthusiastic in the association of saintly people? Are you enthusiastic about what you can experience in your purest state? We must examine our spiritual life on a daily, weekly, and even yearly basis. This examination will help us recognize how various activities and thoughts affect us. We should note how the quality of our experiences varies according to our absorption in the process of *bhakti*.

During this self-analysis, some people find that regulation in their spiritual practices helps maintain enthusiasm because the spiritual activities keep the consciousness absorbed in a positive direction. Other people find that a sense of worth or accomplishment helps them feel enlivened. Most have seen that being properly engaged in service can help increase their focus in God consciousness whereas excessive idle time can lead to apathy. Many notice how associating with other people who also have enthusiasm can increase our own enthusiasm. When we chant, meditate, and pray with those who have a taste for the holy name, it will naturally affect us in a positive way. Some people may notice a distinct relationship between their food intake and level of excitement. Overeating can cause a person to feel slothful and lazy.

On the other hand, we can recognize the times in which we felt more disturbances, doubts, and fears than ever before. Some might find themselves in a state of constant *bhoga-tyaga* or a position of alternating sense enjoyment and renunciation. Some days such a person might feel fixed and other days absorbed in the senses. However, this constant fluctuation will not help us to really become deep *suddha-bhaktas*. We must discover what allows us to maintain enthusiasm instead of seeking a temporary experience of some flickering feeling or sentiment.

These, of course, are just a few ideas to help stimulate your own thought process. We want you to specifically research your own life to see what works for each of you and what does not work. Then, include more of the positive activities in your life. We have to take more control of our spiritual progress. By examining our situations comprehensively, we can find ways to protect and nourish our devotional creeper. Therefore, we want to look deeper into our past and present. We want to do those things that will enhance our spiritual life. Hopefully, each of us knows someone who is enthusiastic most of the time or even all the time. Unfortunately, we also know people who never seem enlivened about life.

Essence of Spiritual Life

What is the essence of all the *vidhi-nisedha* or rules and prohibitions mentioned in the scriptures? The essence of all positive injunctions is to always remember the Lord. This ability to always remember God will lead us to the goal of recognizing Him as our well-wisher, greatest provider, and protector who is very magnanimously inviting all living entities back to their original home in the spiritual kingdom. Therefore, our enthusiasm and activities should assist us in this endeavor to always happily and joyfully think of Krishna. We might engage in so many services and activities, but they should all absorb us in thoughts of the Lord. Of course, the most essential negative injunction is to never forget the Lord.

Keep in mind that the Lord descends for our benefit and His activities help us always think of Him. Krishna and His *saktyavesa-avataras* or empowered incarnations help to enthuse us through their activities—they enable us to increase our anticipation of what we can ultimately experience. The Lord checks things that interfere with our enthusiasm by dealing with the miscreants and establishing genuine religion. Basically, the essence of Vedic *dharma* involves thinking of the Lord and avoiding the opposite. When devotees reflect on the essential aspects of Krishna's descent, it deeply enthuses them and they attain bliss.

Those *brahmanas* who have the commission to chant the Gayatri prayer offer daily respects to the spiritual master, to Lord Caitanya, and to Krishna, acknowledging how they enthuse us to regain our dormant awareness and join the eternal romance. These prayers remind us that we no longer have to accept a lower taste and involve ourselves in lower pleasures that are temporary and end in confusion. Spiritual life involves excitement, which is an integral theme on the spiritual journey. All bona fide scriptures and great teachers give us this message. Spiritual life is adventurous, full of pleasures, and full of variety. It is available for all. These great personalities want to enthuse us to become more and more aware of that reality. They want us to enthusiastically participate in what they are already experiencing.

The Dangers of Apathy

We should never minimize the fact that the ultimate goal is full of pleasure, nor should we minimize the danger of losing enthusiasm. When we find ourselves unenthusiastic, a siren should go off in our consciousness because it opens a door for *maya* to enter. As soon as we lose our enthusiasm, we should realize that *maya* now has the chance to walk right in and cause destruction. When we find ourselves lacking enthusiasm, we must immediately find out how and where the enemies of the mind have attacked us. When these enemies do not attack us, we will feel highly enthusiastic. Can any of us feel enthusiastic while someone grabs, punches, or kicks us? Fear, lust, anger, enviousness, pride, madness, and so on try to assault us, sometimes all at the same time.

The degree of our lack of enthusiasm can indicate the seriousness of the attack. For instance, a doctor can understand the gravity of a disease such as cancer or the flu by looking at the stages and the symptoms already manifesting. Since we understand what constitutes a healthy person, we can also understand what constitutes a diseased person. Similarly, the scriptures and the great *acaryas* or teachers help us understand what constitutes spiritual health. First of all, how much do we always think of the Lord? If we always think of someone who loves and protects us, how can we feel unenthused? Can we really feel apathetic if we know that the person who loves us is the most beautiful, the most knowledgeable, the wealthiest, the most renounced, the most famous, and the strongest? When we deeply accept these profound truths, the enemies of the mind cannot infiltrate and cause a lack of enthusiasm.

We want to avoid the attacks that rob us of enthusiasm because we realize that a lack of enthusiasm means a greater chance of receiving another body. It means that we are not relishing the process or practicing sufficiently what we are to become. No one in the spiritual world feels apathetic. It simply does not exist. Consequently, we cannot return to the spiritual world unless we become like the residents there. We cannot advance in our devotional life if we feel bored, faithless, and depressed. We cannot experience the higher taste when we fill ourselves with anxiety, fear, depression, and grief that even lead some people to suicide. If we overly absorb ourselves in grief and anxiety, it will take our energy and consciousness away from the ecstasy, the *bhava*, and the *prema*.

The senses and the mind must go somewhere. They cannot just remain idle. If we do not properly repose them in spiritual subject matters, they will go in unhealthy directions. We know that we cannot embrace sin and God at the same time. The Bible similarly reminds us, "No one can serve two masters; for either he will hate the one and love the other, or he will be devoted to one and despise the other. You cannot serve God and mammon" (Matthew 6:24). It just cannot happen. You cannot cheat in that way, especially since the Lord is in the heart and He notices everything. Should Krishna welcome us back and make further arrangements for us if He sees that we are not eager to come home? No, He has given us free will. If He sees that we whimsically and lackadaisically engage in the process of *sadhana-bhakti*, we basically send a message to Him and His servants that we do not want to return to the spiritual kingdom. Conversely, if we are excited about the opportunity to serve the Lord, naturally He will reciprocate with even more efficiency. If you are trying to arrange something for a person who doesn't care one way or the other, you will not be as excited to make that arrangement.

Causes of Stagnation

Certain activities and mindsets cause stagnation. The nine tenets of spiritual life include *sravanam* (hearing), *kirtanam* (chanting), *smaranam* (remembering the Lord), *pada-sevanam* (serving the lotus feet of the Lord), *arcanam* (offering the Lord respectful worship), *vandanam* (offering prayers to the Lord), *dasyam* (becoming His servant), *sakhyam* (considering the Lord as one's best friend), and *atma-nivedam* (surrendering everything to Him). We cannot perform these activities enthusiastically without properly aligning our consciousness in devotional life. As a matter of fact, each or all of these will become like laborious tasks. There is no question of *atma-nivedana* or full surrender if we lack enthusiasm or serve nonchalantly. We must move with great intensity in order to break through the modes of material nature. It requires *drdha-vrata* or strong faith and *laulya* or spiritual greed to increase our taste. The taste increases after having an initial sample because we will then want more of the same flavor. When we only have a minimal taste, we will not be as excited to acquire more. We may even doubt that it is possible.

Six Activities Spoil Devotional Service

Many obstacles lead to stagnation on the spiritual path such as *anarthas*, weeds, and the enemies of the mind. In *The Nectar of Instruction*, Text 2, Srila Rupa Gosvami explains:

> *atyaharah prayasas ca*
> *prajalpo niyamagrahah*
> *jana-sangas ca laulyam ca*
> *sadbhir bhaktir vinasyati*
>
> One's devotional service is spoiled when he becomes too entangled in the following six activities: (1) eating more than necessary or collecting more funds than required; (2) overendeavoring for mundane things that are very difficult to obtain; (3) talking unnecessarily about mundane subject matters; (4) practicing the scriptural rules and regulations only for the sake of following them and not for the sake of spiritual advancement, or rejecting the rules and regulations of the scriptures and working independently or whimsically; (5) associating with worldly-minded persons who are not interested in Krishna consciousness; and (6) being greedy for mundane achievements.

As we can see, certain activities cause *vinasyati* or falldown and these activities have some connection with all the enemies of the mind. Let us take *atyahara* for example which means overeating and over-collecting. Someone may be over-collecting because they are envious of a colleague's possessions. They angrily feel that they deserve more than what is coming to them and have the illusion that acquiring material things will totally satisfy them. This lust and greed is causing the person to over-collect, which later makes him experience madness because the more he collects, the more he frustrates others as well as himself. One can never be truly satisfied by pursuing temporary objects. Each of the remaining five categories also rely on the six enemies. One can do their own exercise with each of these to see how they are produced and maintained by the enemies of the mind.

Pause for twenty minutes before proceeding to read further and reflect on ways or possible ways that each category is produced and supported by the enemies of the mind. Study them one by one, first perhaps considering examples relating to yourself and then examples relating to others.

What Hinders Enthusiasm

In the book, *Madhurya-Kadambini*, the author Srila Visvanatha Cakravarti Thakura also gives us six reasons why enthusiasm does not develop properly as he describes the gradations of unsteady devotional service. Again, we want to apply this to our own lives in order to find ways to increase our consistency and enthusiasm in spiritual life.

1. *Utsaha-mayi* or sudden enthusiasm occurs when a neophyte experiences enthusiasm due to the novelty of the spiritual environment. Since the devotee is part of a new process, he or she feels special and full of pride, which enthuses them—for a moment. However, it does not last long. In most cases, when we begin on the path of *bhakti* or on the spiritual journey, Krishna gives us some special experiences and tastes so that

we will have enthusiasm, but it is not steady. Srila Visvanatha Cakravarti explains the reason for *utsaha-mayi* so that we can persevere and maintain enthusiasm beyond this initial stage. We want to make enthusiasm an integral part of our existence rather than just a flickering emotion based on pride and ego.

2. *Ghana-tarala* means that a person is sometimes enthusiastic and sometimes lethargic. We might engage in hearing, chanting, and remembering, but the quality of the service differs as we go through these fluctuations. During the periods of enthusiasm, we find ourselves having more faith and committing less *aparadhas*; consequently, we will have less devastating attacks coming from the enemies of the mind. Conversely, when we fall into the lethargy, the enemies of the mind will mercilessly take their toll.

3. *Vyudha-vikalpa* is a stage in which doubts assail our resolve. Although a person might accept the philosophy to a certain extent, doubts basically outweigh his or her beliefs. The devotee might make commitments and resolutions but suddenly vacillate at the last minute due to lingering doubts. A person will question all of his or her own decisions, consequently failing to come to any conclusion. The individual might ask, "Can I really accept that Krishna has my best interest in mind? What if God does not exist after all? Does this process really work?" These questions create stronger doubts than faith.

4. *Visaya-sangara* is a stage in which the devotee has an internal tug-of-war with material sense enjoyment. The faith has superseded the doubts, but the person still falls victim to *bhoga-tyaga* or a constant fluctuation between enjoyment and renunciation. The attachment to sense gratification is quite strong. In the earlier stages, we still have attachments, but they don't create as many problems as the doubts that pervade our whole existence. Later, we read and understand more of the

philosophy, but our senses and sinful desires overpower us. Although the devotee at this stage now understands right from wrong, the passions lead the person into deviation.

5. *Niyamaksama* is a stage in which the practitioner lacks mature *bhakti*. The doubts and attachments have diminished; however, he or she still lacks the fixed resolve to increase and improve their devotional activities. They make vows and commitments to improve, but, at the last moment, they cannot follow through. They lack high quality devotion.

6. The last stage of unsteady devotion is called *taranga-rangini* in which the devotee still has an attachment to wealth, adoration, and distinction. At this point, the practitioner is almost successful on the path. They are no longer in the position of a neophyte; they have given up *bhoga-tyaga*; they have minimized their doubts; and have risen above mediocre devotion. They have all good qualities, but they fall victim to *pratistha* or pride. Due to their good qualities and deep level of devotion, they naturally attract wealth, adoration, and position. Unfortunately, such by-products check the ultimate experience of the highest level of enthusiasm and love of God.

Six Principles Guarantee Enthusiasm

Rupa Gosvami gives us six principles in Text Three of his *Nectar of Instruction* that guarantee rich *bhakti* and unequivocally guarantee the highest enthusiasm. Of these principles, *utsaha* appears first:

> *utsahan niscayad dhairyat*
> *tat-tat-karma-pravartanat*
> *sanga-tyagat sato vrtteh*
> *sadbhir bhaktih prasidhyati*

There are six principles favorable to the execution of pure devotional service: (1) being enthusiastic, (2) endeavoring with confidence, (3) being patient, (4) acting according to regulative principles such as *sravanam kirtanam visnoh smaranam* or hearing, chanting, and remembering Krishna, (5) abandoning the association of nondevotees, and (6) following in the footsteps of the previous *acaryas*. These six principles undoubtedly assure the complete success of pure devotional service.

1. **Being enthusiastic**—If we lack this sense of zeal in our lives, we might as well begin to prepare for another material body because it means that the enemy has captured us. After the enemy has attacked, do we allow it to destroy us completely or do we do take the necessary steps to eliminate it?

2. **Endeavoring with confidence**—If we lack confidence, we will not follow guru, *sadhu*, and *sastra* with intensity or perseverance. This will cause us to speculate and eventually deviate.

3. **Being patient**—Enthusiasm and excitement mean that we greatly anticipate the possibilities, but, at the same time, we must also be patient. How do these two mindsets coincide? On the one hand, if we lack patience while endeavoring with this intense enthusiasm, we will deny

Krishna's position as the Supreme Controller. Instead of recognizing the ways in which Krishna is facilitating us, we will become angry when certain arrangements do not manifest according to our own particular time. On the other hand, if we patiently wait for the Lord's mercy without acting enthusiastically, our consciousness will not be strong or protected sufficiently to keep out the enemies of the mind. We will begin to doubt whether or not the goal is worth the endeavor. Actually, we must be enthusiastic and spiritually greedy while being patient. We must eagerly serve in an emergency consciousness while never failing to realize that Krishna and His servants are making all arrangements for us according to time, place, and circumstance. For instance, in the workplace, a person works hard at his or her job with confidence that the employer will reciprocate with the appropriate payment. He knows that the promised check will come if he simply perseveres. This can help explain the seeming contradiction between enthusiasm and patience.

4. **Acting according to the regulative principles**—The regulative principles are our medicine. If a sick person is properly diagnosed, the medicine and treatment prescribed are essential in helping restore the person to normalcy. The regulative principles are prescribed by our *acaryas* and are essential for our welfare.

5. **Abandoning the association of nondevotees**—While moving with haste on the spiritual path, we must be careful about the influence of those who have fallen into depression, stagnation, guilt, anger, anxiety, and into the many other corollaries of the enemies of the mind. If you

are fighting a war and your fellow soldier has become a coward or a spy for the adversary, can you comfortably associate with that person, revealing your mind and heart? The person has turned into an agent of the enemy. Similarly, if you spend time with someone who has a contagious disease, you would obviously be extremely careful. Therefore, this instruction is just a practical consideration. In order to achieve, we must be very careful about our associations.

6. **Following in the footsteps of the previous acaryas**—We want to study the examples of those who have come before us and succeeded on the path of *bhakti*. We want to follow them but not imitate them.

All of these six items will produce the pure devotional experience infused with the culture of *bhakti*. Misdirected enthusiasm gets a person into trouble, but properly directed enthusiasm helps us control the mind and senses rather than serve them helplessly. The purport to this particular text in the *Nectar of Instruction* follows:

> One should accept this opportunity to return home, back to Godhead, very enthusiastically. Without enthusiasm, one cannot be successful. Even in the material world one has to be very enthusiastic in his particular field of activity in order to become successful. A student, businessman, artist or anyone else who wants success in his line must be enthusiastic. Similarly, one has to be

very enthusiastic in devotional service. Enthusiasm means action, but action for whom? The answer is that one should always act for Krishna.

Endeavor executed with intelligence in Krishna consciousness is called *utsaha,* or enthusiasm. The devotees find the correct means by which everything can be utilized in the service of the Lord (*nirbandhah krsna-sambandhe yuktam vairagyam ucyate*). The execution of devotional service is not a matter of idle meditation but practical action in the foreground of spiritual life.

We cannot consistently honor any of these principles without enthusiasm. Our level of enthusiasm can function as a barometer to determine our progress.

Symptoms of Success

Nine activities begin to dominate a devotee's life when he or she reaches the stage of *bhava* or devotional ecstasy. At this stage, the practitioner has already passed through the previous stages known as *sraddha* (faith), *sadhu-sanga* (association with devotees), *bhajana-kriya* (practicing devotional service under the guidance of a spiritual master), *anartha-nivrtti* (the removal of unwanted obstacles and offenses), *nistha* (steadiness), *ruci* (strong taste for spiritual activities), and *asakti* (intense attachment to the Lord). After *asakti*, the devotee reaches the stage of *bhava*, which comes before *prema* or the highest perfected stage of life. *Bhava* can only manifest after passing through these necessary stages since *bhava* cannot develop without steadiness and steadiness cannot develop without constant enthusiasm.

Imagine taking an elevator from the first floor all the way up to the penthouse. A person has to pass all the different levels, but then the door opens and leads into the penthouse. We might compare that open door to *bhava* or ecstasy which is pushing away all other unhealthy blocks and *anarthas* once and for all. At this stage, the aspirant goes through final cleansings that allow the soul to walk into the spiritual realm and experience the *prema*. Consequently, we want to look at the symptoms of the person who has reached the door and witness the effects of enthusiasm. Arjuna similarly inquired into this topic in the *Bhagavad-gita*, asking Krishna how such a person who has transcended material nature walks, talks, and in general behaves. How can we recognize such a person and what does he or she experience? Below are some of the symptoms given by the *acaryas* of one who is transcending material nature and knocking on the door of *prema*. Such a person is situated in *bhava*.

1. *Avyartha-kalatvam*—utilization of time in the service of the Lord. How do we use our own time? When we don't use our time efficiently, the enemies of the mind definitely become more active.

2. *Ksanti*—perseverance or the ability to remain tolerant even amid disturbance. This compares to Rupa Gosvami's second tenet of firm conviction; that is, endeavoring with determination.

3. *Virakti*—detachment from the objects of sense enjoyment. We do not want to be void of enthusiasm nor do we want to attach ourselves to unhealthy enthusiasm. We have to detach ourselves from the unhealthy in order to access the healthy.

4. *Mana-sunyata*—pridelessness. Pride is a serious enemy, which blocks the ecstasy. Humility is an antibiotic that checks the enemies of the mind from spreading or even surfacing.

5. *Asa-bandha*—hope against hope that the Lord will bestow His causeless mercy on the individual. Even when the obstacles seem insurmountable and intense, it doesn't stop an enthusiastic person. Such a person has a natural mood of optimism, trying to use whatever is happening in their lives for growth and service. They will find a way to get around any obstacle or difficulty and will not allow it to impose in any way on them by causing them to think of themselves as a failure.

6. *Samutkantha*—intense eagerness to serve the Lord. It does not matter where they are, who they are with, what opulences they have, or what they lack, such devotees are always intensely eager to experience pure love of God.

7. *Nama-gane sada ruci*—constant attraction to chanting the holy names of the Lord. The devotee at this stage of *bhava* has a strong attachment to call on the Lord. They constantly find ways to prepare themselves for the experience by constantly remembering the highest goal. In order to reach the goal, they understand that they have to position

themselves to receive it. Such devotees accomplish this by trying to attract the attention of those who can bring blessings and grace upon an individual.

8. *Asaktis tad-gunakhyane*—addiction to glorifying and speaking about the qualities of the Lord. By glorifying the *lilas* or pastimes of the Lord, they will gradually rise to a level in which they can participate.

9. *Pritis tad-vasati sthale*—eager to live in the holy places where the Lord has performed His pastimes. A person standing at the door has already passed through the necessary prerequisites and has the ability to soon join the eternal associates of the Lord in the spiritual kingdom. They are enthusiastic about living in the holy places of pilgrimage because they are ready for the experience and do not want to wait until they leave the physical body. Although they still reside in a material body, they are taking shelter of spiritual environments in order to absorb themselves more in the spiritual culture. It provides a natural protection from apathy and unhealthy association. In the spiritual environment, they can walk around and reside in the places where some of the Lord's pastimes have taken place. Therefore, it becomes the rightful claim of such a person to walk right through that special door.

Pastimes from the Scriptures

Endless examples of great personalities experiencing these states of ecstasy exist in the scriptures. They constantly experience transcendental enthusiasm due to *vipralambha* (separation) and then *sambhoga* (association). This culminates in the natural activities of the soul who is enthusiastically involved in all kinds of adventures, associations, and experiences. Spiritual life has always been about happiness and enthusiasm. We will not find any boredom, depression, anxiety, or gloom in the kingdom of God. If we experience all of these setbacks related to the enemies of the mind, it indicates that we are not yet candidates to knock on the door of *prema*. *Bhava* is the key due to enthusiasm and ecstasy, which arises as a result of shedding unhealthy *anarthas*. The person can finally experience their authentic self. The following are stories from the Vedic texts, which share some pastimes of enthusiasm.

The Perfect Offering

Vidura, a pure devotee of the Lord, invited Krishna to his small cottage to stay during His trip to Hastinapura. The Lord chose to stay in the small cottage of His dear devotee rather than in the big palace of Duhsasana. During His stay, Vidura felt such intense enthusiasm and excitement to have Krishna's association that instead of offering Krishna the intended banana, he offered the banana peel instead. In his state of love and ecstasy, he did not even realize his mistake. How did Krishna respond? Due to Vidura's intense love and eagerness, the Lord accepted the banana peel with great pleasure and relished the offering. He accepted an offering from His *suddha-bhakta* or pure devotee with enthusiasm. When we have this kind of enthusiasm, Krishna fully reciprocates. Even if we make an offering that seems to lack the greatest skill or perfection, it is successful due to the love.

The Love of a Devotee

Sudama, a poor *brahmana* who went to school with

Krishna in his youth, was encouraged by his wife to approach the Lord for some help in their poverty stricken situation. When he finally entered in the association of the Lord, he was so full of enthusiasm just to gaze upon Him that he entirely forgot to ask for help. He simply felt fulfilled to have the association of his dear friend. However, Krishna was so enthusiastic to once again see His childhood friend that He gave him exorbitant wealth and opulences. Krishna always fulfills His promise, which He makes in *Bhagavad-gita* 9.22:

> *ananyas cintayanto mam*
> *ye janah paryupasate*
> *tesam nityabhiyuktanam*
> *yoga-ksemam vahamy aham*

> But those who always worship Me with exclusive devotion, meditating on My transcendental form—to them I carry what they lack, and I preserve what they have.

He is always ready to help us if we are ready to receive.

Beyond Limitations

In 1893, Jagannatha dasa Babaji, a great Vaisnava saint and renunciate, was traveling to various places of pilgrimage. In these final stages of his life, his servants had to carry him everywhere for he could no longer walk. However, when he reached the presumed birth site of Lord Caitanya, which Bhaktivinoda Thakura had previously discovered, he jumped up and began to dance in ecstasy. He became empowered far beyond his actual physical capacity and of course confirmed the authenticity of the site for all Vaisnavas. Enthusiasm can cause us to far surpass our normal capacity.

Enthusiastic Ecstasy

The *gopis* have obviously far surpassed the stage of *bhava*, but their examples can help us understand where enthusiasm can ultimately lead us. They can give us a vision of the amazing activities in the spiritual world in which every moment is a greater chance to enthusiastically give love to the Divine Couple and receive love from Them.

> The appearance of the moon increased Krsna's desire to dance with the gopis. The forests were filled with fragrant flowers. The atmosphere was cooling and festive. When Lord Krsna began to blow His flute, the gopis all over Vrndavana became enchanted. Their attraction to the vibration of the flute increased a thousand times due to the rising full moon, the red horizon, the calm and cool atmosphere and the blossoming flowers. All these gopis were by nature very much attracted to Krsna's beauty, and when they heard the vibration of His flute, they became apparently lustful to satisfy the senses of Krsna.
>
> Immediately upon hearing the vibration of the flute, they all left their respective engagements and proceeded to the spot where Krsna was standing.

> While they ran very swiftly, all their earrings swung back and forth. They all rushed toward the place known as Vamsivata. Some of them were engaged in milking cows, but they left their milking business half finished and immediately went to Krishna.

In our rural projects for instance, we should milk the cows and take care of the farms with enthusiasm that we are anticipating the sound of Krishna's ankle bells and flute. We want to execute our services with anticipation, knowing that Krishna can reveal the spiritual world to us due to our deep quality of devotion. Our intense enthusiasm can connect with His enthusiasm to receive us.

> One of them had just collected milk and put it in a milk pan on the stove to boil, but she did not care whether the milk overboiled and spilled -- she immediately left to go see Krsna. Some of them were breast-feeding their small babies, and some were engaged in distributing food to the members of their families, but they left all such engagements and immediately rushed towards the spot where Krsna was playing His flute.

Even if we are not engaged in physical service, we should still engage in *mana-seva* or devotional service within the mind at all times. We should always anticipate Krishna's invitation so that when He actually invites us, we run towards Him. If our minds are not properly absorbed, we will not hear the call or we will be too occupied with other distractions, missing the chance to engage in deep service to the Lord.

> Some were engaged in serving their husbands, and some were themselves engaged in eating, but caring neither to serve their husbands nor eat, they immediately left. Some of them wanted to decorate their faces with cosmetic ointments and to dress themselves very nicely before going to Krsna, but unfortunately they could not finish their cosmetic decorations or put on their clothes in the right way because of their anxiety to meet Krsna immediately. Their faces were decorated hurriedly and were haphazardly finished; some even put the lower part of their clothes on the upper part of their bodies and the upper part on the lower part.[8]

Even while we eat, we must practice mindfulness. If Krishna calls, will we say, "Just wait one minute until I finish this cheesecake. I'll come a little later." No, even our eating should be a form of meditation and service in which we honor the Lord's remnants. When Krishna calls, will we say, "I will go but let me first fix my bangles." No, when the call comes, we want to spontaneously run towards our Lord. We do not want to be so absorbed in making money for Krishna that we do not hear the call. We make money, but we should make it in the proper consciousness. While offering an *arati* or worship to the Lord, we don't want to be so absorbed in each item or in the number of circles that we cannot hear Krishna call for us. We must accelerate both the external and internal counterparts for the proper acceleration of enthusiasm. All of the *gopis'* activities and words revolve entirely around the service of Krishna; therefore, when He calls, they do not have to waste a single minute, indecisively wondering what to do. Since they perpetually offer all of their activities to Krishna, nothing can distract them from entering fully into His association.

Run Enthusiastically Towards the Door

These great personalities have such a high level of enthusiasm that nothing can distract them from the service of the Lord. We want to accelerate our own consciousness by removing any distractions, which interfere with our progressive march toward this ultimate goal. It does not mean that we should be in denial, but it means that we do not let anything dominate our consciousness other than service to the Lord. Doubts, attachments, and other enemies of the mind will all prevent us from experiencing this ultimate joy and excitement. Even a person who worries too much about their own weaknesses and faults will also lack sufficient determination because all of their energy will go into these negative reflections. As confirmed in *Srimad-Bhagavatam* 10.14.58, the material world is a place of misery and danger at every step: *padam padam yad vipadam na tesam*. Therefore, we don't want to put all our energy into this realm.

Everyone has the opportunity to come to the door, which leads to *prema*. We want to reach that door ourselves while also bringing as many people as possible. We don't want to delay our own return because somebody else has lost their enthusiasm. We want to be carriers of enthusiasm to such an extent that we can infect others, but if we cannot infect others with our enthusiasm, we certainly do not want other people to drain us, ruining our own chance to escape into the realm of eternal joy and excitement.

Questions and Answers

Question: At different points during our spiritual growth, we may reach plateaus where we have to work out specific issues before we can continue on our progressive march. When we reach these plateaus, do the tests affect our enthusiasm, and if so, how can we protect our enthusiasm and determination?

Answer: A devotee who is actually serious will have very temporary bouts of confusion, but it will not really zap them of their enthusiasm. Instead, they will see these challenges as chances to confront the enemy in battle and win. The enemy has been exposed which increases their enthusiasm even more. It means that the attacks of the mind will not disturb a high level devotee. Some temporary jolt may occur, but it will not drastically disturb them. They will see it as a chance to address their fear, false ego, or lust. It pushes them to reach higher levels of acceleration. On the other hand, a low achiever or a person suffering from low self-esteem will meet the enemy who will simply overwhelm them due to their lack of faith.

God is directly and indirectly responsible for everything that happens to each person. Therefore, if we get upset about something in our lives, it has to do with some lack of faith in the Supreme Lord. For this reason, we emphasized the importance of being active, aggressive, and enthusiastic while simultaneously being patient. We want to actively cover our part of the contract while waiting for the Lord to cover His part of the contract—on His own time. We have patience because we have faith that He will do what He has promised.

Although our spiritual progression is not always vertical, this does not deter a person who really understands the science of self-realization. They just try to see how each arrangement is a manifestation of the Lord's mercy. Since the Lord has given us mercy in a particular way, we want to take advantage of it and use it for our growth. If we remain enthusiastic, we will come out on the other side as a much more realized and potent person. Basically, we never have any justification for a lack of enthusiasm. Even if we have the most awesome challenges, we have the ability to be enthusiastic and learn. We never have a legitimate reason for apathy. This basically sums up the essence of this entire topic.

Question: In the beginning, you described two types of people—those with misdirected enthusiasm and those who do not have any enthusiasm. Can we also have misdirected enthusiasm within spiritual life?

Answer: Definitely. For instance, we have heard Rupa Gosvami's injunction against over-endeavoring for mundane things that are very difficult to attain. A person on the spiritual path can still strive for the wrong goals. *Pratistha* or the desire for profit, distinction, and adoration also misleads devotees into serving for the satisfaction of their own ego. The devotee might serve so enthusiastically but only to receive honor and fame. These are just a few examples of misdirected enthusiasm.

When a devotee falls victim to these traps, Krishna might help him or her by arranging the exact opposite. Instead of honor, the person might receive great dishonor which can ultimately help them understand how to not only engage in devotional service, but to serve in the right way as well. However, if a person does not have sufficient association and faith, they will want to give up when Krishna takes away the reward. We must come to the point of unconditional and unmotivated devotional service in order to knock on the door of *prema*. Krishna might facilitate us by giving us honor, but when He considers us mature enough, He will take it away to see if we still eagerly serve without the reward.

For instance, in a relationship, two lovers reciprocate in many different ways by offering service, care, and attention. However, if one person withdraws some of their service and attentiveness, does that mean the other person will also stop or does the second person continue to steadily give love in order to arrive at a sweeter level of association? Similarly, Krishna might reciprocate in some initial ways, but when He seemingly stops, He will take notice to see the actual depth of our love. Are we serving mainly to obtain the opulences of God or do we really want to develop genuine love? This is the main problem among those engaged in *yoga-misra-bhakti*, *karma-misra-bhakti*, or *jnana-misra-bhakti*. The *bhakti* is mixed with fruitive activities, knowledge, or *yoga*; therefore, it is not completely pure.

Question: Can enthusiasm itself become misdirected? If we only serve the Lord when we feel a certain emotion, it could keep us on the conditional platform. It seems that in order to reach the level of complete surrender, we must be able to continue with our service even when we lack taste and enthusiasm.

Answer: One may then ask, "If we never have a legitimate reason to feel unenthusiastic, why has the Lord given us the process of *sadhana-bhakti*?" In the beginning, we mainly serve out of duty rather than out of enthusiasm and we often feel more excited when we can work according to our propensity. However, if we seriously want to make spiritual advancement, we will find a way to enthusiastically do our service even if we do not have a propensity for that type of work.

We might even be able to work in such a way that our propensities come out. For instance, a person might have to do business and function as a *vaisya* although they really feel more comfortable with the activities of a *brahmana*. If this person has a sufficient level of enthusiasm, they might find a way to dovetail their brahminical tendencies by teaching business because they will see it as an opportunity given by Krishna. They are not denying their propensity; rather, they are going deeper into whatever situation the Lord arranges. Therefore, the person finds ways to dovetail their brahminical tendencies even in this field of business. They might make money as a teacher by offering workshops and courses and maintain their enthusiasm even though they are seemingly outside of their natural tendency.

We certainly do not want to imply that a person should only do what feels good because many things feel good that are in no way spiritual. The Lord might send a particular situation that is outside of our natural grain, but if we persevere, it can help us move through the door towards *prema*. What might seem to be an obstacle could really be a chance to come closer to the Supreme Personality of Godhead.

Whatever duty we have, we want to do it with intensity while praying to the Lord for the ability to offer it with greater love and effectiveness. In this way, we will gradually move away from acting merely out of duty. For instance, I came to a community in Pennsylvania to help revive it as a service to my spiritual master. I knew this would be his desire. My own preference would have been to stay in the city or to start a totally fresh rural project in a different area. However, because I accepted the service out of duty, I tried to find more and more ways to absorb myself. By my spiritual mentor's mercy, I have become so excited about this project. I never thought I would find myself in a rural area, especially in a town in the middle of nowhere, but now I can barely wait to return after every trip. During my travels all around the world, I begin to feel enthused at the end of a trip when I can come back to this beautiful 400-acre farm community. Now I do most of my writing here. I accepted out of duty but then tried to go deeper into it by appreciating my chance to make an offering.

At times, we may not particularly like a service, but we should not restrict ourselves only to just the services that inspire us at that moment. However, we should never feel comfortable when we lack enthusiasm. We should try to be enthusiastic based on the situation, which will naturally lead to richer and healthier enthusiasm. Basically, the modes of material nature cover us and they unfold in all kinds of ways to create enemies, blocks, *anarthas*, and stagnations. When we have an intense desire for what is available, we will break through. But we must remember that we cannot be intense without firm conviction and perseverance, which means enthusiasm.

Interestingly, some of the devotees in our society who put the most energy into health also suffer from the most intense bouts of sickness. We can put so much time and energy into our health that we miss the chance to live fully in the moment. We might even create more sicknesses because of our intense focus in that area. It becomes an obsession. We know that eventually the body does deteriorate, but how much more cumbersome to have physical complications while simultaneously worrying about it each day to the point of lamentation. We worry and take action but then leave the results up to the Lord.

Question: When we go through periods in which we lack enthusiasm, should we see it as an austerity of the mind that can strengthen us to ultimately break through the challenge? Otherwise, if we only look for those things that feel good, we run away from the austerity of the mind that will make us strong. It seems that it would be better to persevere during those times even when we lack enthusiasm.

Answer: We are not masochists or sadists. We do not enjoy suffering nor do we purposely look for situations that will make us suffer. The *Bhagavad-gita* places this type of austerity in the mode of ignorance. However, strength does develop from austerity. We do observe that spiritualists who keep trying to adjust their lives for comfort simply wind up frustrated. Devotees who whimsically give up services when difficulties arise end up hating themselves, hating others, and even doubting Krishna. People who just try to find some pleasure within devotional service for themselves and who never go out of their comfort zones will never really be comfortable. The ecstasy comes from utilizing time and going beyond the ordinary to access the extraordinary. God is far beyond the ordinary.

Reflect on times in your own life when you took more of a risk for the Lord, involving yourself in pioneering work. Notice how you felt more God conscious. Some of the householders are at a point in their lives in which most of their meditation goes into maintenance. Although such endeavors are needed, some might remain too absorbed in this stage. When this happens, notice how you feel drier. Risk-taking involves austerity. The risk compares to a little child who jumps off the top step into the mother's arms. Since the parents love their children, the parents are there to catch them when they take that risk. Similarly, when we take that risk in the service of the Supreme, He is already there to help us. It is only scary when, due to our doubts, we wonder if the Supreme Lord will really catch us if we take that jump.

We do not want to be foolish, but we **do** want to go beyond the ordinary. The whole discussion emphasizes the importance of taking advantage of opportunities, maintaining our enthusiasm, and avoiding that which will hamper our excitement. It means action with conscientiousness, but, in the background, it really depends on the quality and amount of faith that we have. Faithlessness is one of the causes of apathy. When we have great faith, it will naturally increase our enthusiasm. Basically, when we have too many bouts of lack of enthusiasm, it is not really a lack of enthusiasm, but actually a lack of faith. Lack of faith brings mental dullness and a lack of proper action, which then leads to a lack of mercy. We actually get more mercy when our faith is stronger which also means that our enthusiasm will be stronger. Therefore, we will more eagerly and comprehensively engage in healthy activities. Ironically, when we are unenthusiastic, we want more mercy but it does not come in that way.

Although we want enthusiasm, we also should not be in denial or artificial about our situation. Instead, we should look closer at what we need to fix. We should acknowledge that we are suffering but then ask for help. We might have doubts or have trouble in our relationships, which we sometimes need to express, but we share so that another person can help us develop more enthusiasm. In this way, we reveal our hearts and minds.

The Necessity of Enthusiasm

Question: As you explained, we are not masochistic and we understand the importance of balance, but whose responsibility is it to seek that balance? Is it the responsibility of the individual, the authorities, the guru, or do we wait for Krishna to intervene?

Answer: All of these aspects are crucial. It's our responsibility to pursue service, to follow spiritual principles, to chant the holy name, to pray, and to help and serve others. We should repose our energy in all of these areas. After all of our endeavors to arrange, organize, or manage, the essence of spiritual life is to depend on Krishna's mercy so that He can amplify our endeavors or let it all fall apart. The *svarupa-laksana* or the greatest quality of a Vaisnava is his or her full dependence on the Lord.

However, depending on mercy does not mean that we should be inactive, independent, or dull. It means that we should be interdependent. If we are dependent, solely waiting for Krishna's mercy to manifest, we will wait for 8,400,000 additional lifetimes. If we are independent and doubt the availability of the mercy, we will fail because we cannot conquer *maya* only on our own intelligence and power. *Maya* loves people who fall into this trap. In other words, we should have firm faith and intense eagerness to do our best while leaving the results up to Krishna. We do what is necessary to come to the door and then patiently wait for the mercy and ability to walk through the door. Krishna will do His part to open the door and escort us in.

It is difficult but not complicated. For this reason, we have *sadhu*, *sastra*, and guru. Any time we have a doubt, we must check with all three of these authorities. If we have checked with all of them but then make a mistake, a responsibility is also on them. If we did not check with *sadhu*, *sastra*, and guru and simply used our own intelligence, we will have all kinds of problems. Furthermore, if we doubt the power of *maya*, we will also have a problem. If we get an immature instruction from a bona fide *sadhu*, some lack of clarity from the *sastra*, and seemingly get an ineffective instruction from guru, then it falls on them as well. The responsibility rests with all parties. But if they are proper, Krishna will let the blessings come through because we have acted according to the proper authorities.

While making my decision to come to the rural community in Pennsylvania, I had many reasons to justify not accepting this responsibility. I had a different plan in mind and had many reasons to justify my decision after checking with *sadhu* and *sastra*, but I then had to place it at the feet of my spiritual master. Since I could not justify it, I accepted this service. Consequently, even if I do not excel as much as I would like, it is still not a serious problem because I am acting under proper direction.

If we do not have sufficient faith in *sadhu*, *sastra*, and guru, then of course we will act without their sanction because we will not take the instructions seriously. Consequently, this will dictate some of our activities and failures, which will cause a lack of enthusiasm and a lack of spiritual growth. Nowadays, especially with computer technology, we can find quotes and references from the scripture to support any topic. Furthermore, there are so many varieties of Vaisnavas with all different levels of realization and orientation. Whatever you want to do or say, you can find some group of people who will support you. In this way, it can be very difficult to reach a final conclusion.

As long as we have a personal guru, we have to check with him, and when that guru gives us instructions, we should use our intelligence to see how to intelligently follow. If he somehow gives us a wrong instruction, we are still covered. Of course, if he gives us an instruction that opposes bona fide principles of spiritual life or if he deviates in some way, obviously we shouldn't follow. But if he is connected to the *parampara* and following the instructions of his bona fide mentor, we have a duty to follow his or her instructions and Krishna has the duty to give us blessings. Otherwise, Krishna would be a liar. If we follow the process that Krishna has given us, He has promised us He will give all necessary facilitation.

It is really about the Lord and the living entity. If we have more faith in the Supreme, He will continue to manifest in our lives in so many ways. We will constantly feel enthused. The Lord will even come through the words of a drunken man. We might hear the drunk say something so profound that we gain tremendous insight. For instance, in the *Srimad-Bhagavatam*, we hear of the *avadhuta brahmana* who learned from so many different types of gurus such as the python, the elephants, the bees, and so on. Just by watching ants work together, we can learn about cooperation. We will learn from the cows, peacocks, and so many other living entities. The difficulty really stems from lack of faith in *sadhu*, *sastra*, and guru. Unfortunately, we have trouble in all of these areas and the Lord knows. Therefore, He has given us this process in Kali-yuga of focusing on chanting the names of God for internal as well as external consciousness-raising so that we can still grow in spite of the doubts and weaknesses and continue to nourish our devotional creeper.

For this reason, Rupa Gosvami and Visvanatha Cakravarti give us of all these warnings so that we can avoid that which will destroy our enthusiasm and entire spiritual lives. They give us this whole list of *anarthas*, weeds, and *aparadhas*. No one who has a serious connection with my ministry should be very confused in this area because I focus so much on *anartha-nivrtti* or the removal of unwanted weeds, bad habits, etc. Someone might even run away from my association because I always talk about what to avoid. Some may wonder why I don't talk about higher spiritual experiences more, but when we do overcome *anarthas*, nothing is left but the higher. The *anarthas* or weeds are the only blocks preventing us from experiencing the higher tastes and experiences.

Of course, we must always hear about the spiritual world and the pastimes of the Lord because this creates enthusiasm. We do not want to minimize the importance hearing about the goal, but we must also know what to avoid. Since the modes of material nature have us bound up, it is more important to hear how to get out. For this reason, Srila Prabhupada continuously emphasizes basic philosophy. Again and again he reminds us of the basic fact that we are not our bodies, but ultimately spiritual beings using material bodies. Just hearing about the higher will not set us free if we do not know how to get out of the lower. We cannot skip the whole process starting with *sraddha* and ending with *prema*. The *acaryas* have explained the basic steps to us that we must follow, and as we have discussed in this chapter, one of the most important tenets is maintaining enthusiasm!

Chapter 5

The Need for Constant Mindfulness

> *yato yato niscalati*
> *manas cancalam asthiram*
> *tatas tato niyamyaitad*
> *atmany eva vasam nayet*

From wherever the mind wanders due to its flickering and unsteady nature, one must certainly withdraw it and bring it back under the control of the self.
  Bhagavad-gita 6.26

Recognize the Essence

The practice of mindfulness enables us to perceive the essence of all things. Every entity and element has its *dharma* or essential nature, but the ultimate essence of everything is the Supreme Personality of Godhead. Furthermore, the Godhead is so mystically creative, cleverly subtle, and extraordinarily diverse that recognizing and honoring Him at every moment requires great mindfulness. In other words, mindfulness means to constantly see Krishna or God in everything at all times. It involves the recognition of God's right to be what He wants, when He wants, and interact with us as He likes.

Once the Supreme Lord takes personal interest in our lives, He also reserves the right to teach or benefit us through hard knocks or through gentle means. On our part, we must remember to mindfully see His hand operating at all times, not only when we practice the rituals or associate with spiritual people, but constantly and unceasingly. The challenge is to remain fixed in mindfulness of God always and function in ways that will constantly enhance our vision of Him. In this way, we can gradually begin to sustain a state of *samadhi* or spiritual trance regardless of the external environment.

We sometimes hear of people who continually enter into deeper and deeper states of consciousness or who have the ability to understand things from a deeper perspective. In times to come, such abilities will become increasingly more valuable because as world affairs shift, economies collapse, and troubles increase, people who lack the ability to dive deeper into the transcendental state and experience life at a more profound level will find themselves extremely compromised and disconcerted. Some may even experience such depression that it leads them to the point of suicide. Furthermore, as the advertisers

The Need for Constant Mindfulness 151

increase the hype about sense gratification and the many fantasies of utopia, more people will find it impossible to endure the level of disappointment that life will dish out to them unless they start to perceive spiritual phenomena and tangible confirmations of the existence of God.

People who are unable to go beyond mere religiosity and bathe in spirituality will fail to make deep spiritual connections. Consequently, they will be swept up by the waves of material culture, by demonic propaganda, and by the tremendous illusions that bring all kinds of gloom, anxieties and frustrations. In order to avoid these devastating consequences, we want to focus on how to see God everywhere. Krishna Himself tells us in the *Bhagavad-gita* 10.10:

tesam satata-yuktanam
bhajatam priti-purvakam
dadami buddhi-yogam tam
yena mam upayanti te

To those who are constantly devoted to serving Me with love, I give the understanding by which they can come to Me.

As we have mentioned several times in *Spiritual Warrior IV* and in this book, Krishna also advises His devotees to fully absorb themselves in His worship in the *Bhagavad-gita* 9.34:

man-mana bhava mad-bhakto
mad-yaji mam namaskuru
mam evaisyasi yuktvaivam
atmanam mat-parayanah

> Engage your mind always in thinking of Me, become My devotee, offer obeisances unto Me and worship Me. Being completely absorbed in Me, surely you will come to Me.

Krishna, who is God Himself, tells us to think of Him constantly. God is an infallible source whose advice is much more important than the advice of consultants, coaches, or other resourceful materials.

Krishna actually tells us which thoughts and ideas should occupy our minds. However, after receiving such valid instructions, how does a person execute them? How is it possible to always remain God conscious and always think of the Lord? Although a seemingly improbable goal, this constant remembrance of God is ultimately the essence of spiritual life. When we develop the ability to always think about the Supreme Personality of Godhead along with His name, form, pastimes, activities, servants, and messages of love, then we will gradually enter into the Lord's arena and, in many cases, we will quickly come to a point of directly experiencing God's blessings. All that auspiciousness arises from the mere act of simply reflecting on God, particularly when action follows that contemplation.

The Opulences of God

In the *Bhagavad-gita*, Krishna describes His all pervasiveness in several different verses, and in the seventh chapter He explains how everything rests upon Him:

> *mattah parataram nanyat*
> *kincid asti dhananjaya*
> *mayi sarvam idam protam*
> *sutre mani-gana iva*

> O conqueror of wealth, there is no truth superior to Me. Everything rests upon Me, as pearls are strung on a thread.
> *Bhagavad-gita* 7.7

Here the Lord confirms that all things ultimately rest on Him. This includes all objects, all beings, all emotions, all knowledge, all activities, all attitudes, and all resources—everything rests on and emanates from the Supreme. We want to develop continual mindfulness so that we can experience and interact more with God at every moment. When we develop proper mindfulness, even our external circumstances will no longer matter because we will have dovetailed our consciousness with God and developed cognizance of Him, even at work, at home, or on the street.

In *Bhagavad-gita* 7.6, Krishna continues to explain:

> *etad-yonini bhutani*
> *sarvanity upadharaya*
> *aham krtsnasya jagatah*
> *prabhavah pralayas tatha*

> All created beings have their source in these two natures. Of all that is material and all that is spiritual in this world, know for certain that I am both the origin and the dissolution.

Mindfulness again means experiencing God everywhere, seeing everything as a manifestation of Him, and seeing everything in Him. It also means positioning ourselves to receive and experience God's blessings and auspicious energies. In our day-to-day functions, as we eat, drink, sleep, mate, and defend, we can see all things in relation to Krishna by remembering His words:

> *raso 'ham apsu kaunteya*
> *prabhasmi sasi-suryayoh*
> *pranavah sarva-vedesu*
> *sabdah khe paurusam nrsu*

> O son of Kunti, I am the taste of water, the light of the sun and the moon, the syllable *om* in the Vedic *mantras;* I am the sound in ether and ability in man.
> *Bhagavad-gita* 7.8

Krishna gives us so many opportunities to remember Him. When we observe the sun moving in space, we can immediately reflect on this fiery planet as the eye of God. This simple conception of Krishna's presence can accompany us in our daily dealings and even provide comfort if we act properly because we know that God sees all our efforts to befriend and obey Him.

Most importantly, all of these representations are expressions of God's love for us. Krishna radiates His love in the form of sunshine, which heals, purifies, soothes, and illuminates. If we can remember this fact and allow that thought to permeate throughout our consciousness, then our love of the Supreme will naturally grow without impediments because we will feel intense gratitude for His provisions and protection. Once we enter into this frame of mind, we will find it easier to follow the recommendations of the Vedic scriptures by giving rapt aural reception to the words of God, which are both edifying and pacifying.

When Krishna says, "I am...the light of the sun and the moon, the syllable *om* in the Vedic *mantras*; I am the sound in ether and ability in man," we can recognize His presence more fully, minute by minute. While appreciating the various abilities in a man or woman, we can recognize the Supreme as the source of those talents. Actually, whenever we witness some great achievement, ability, attribute, or beauty, instead of allowing the temporary possessor of that gift to distract us, we can remember the Lord who possesses these brilliant qualities in full. We can also remember His extreme generosity and magnanimity in sharing them so liberally with others.

Furthermore, the act of dispensing these charities to His children, friends, and lovers never depletes or lessens Him in any way. Krishna Himself says:

> *yad yad vibhutimat sattvam*
> *srimad urjitam eva va*
> *tat tad evavagaccha tvam*
> *mama tejo-'msa-sambhavam*
> *atha va bahunaitena*
> *kim jnatena tavarjuna*
> *vistabhyaham idam krtsnam*
> *ekamsena sthito jagat*

> Know that all opulent, beautiful and glorious creations spring from but a spark of My splendor. But what need is there, Arjuna, for all this detailed

knowledge? With a single fragment of Myself I pervade and support this entire universe.
>   *Bhagavad-gita* 10.41-42

When we function with a mindful consciousness during our daily duties at home or at work which may seem quite tedious and unfulfilling, such duties can take on a whole different perspective because we see them in relationship to some aspect of the Creator.

Those of us who are captivated by the wonderful aroma of various scents can relish the Lord in this form. He again states in the *Bhagavad-gita* 7.9:

> *punyo gandhah prthivyam ca*
> *tejas casmi vibhavasau*
> *jivanam sarva-bhutesu*
> *tapas casmi tapasvisu*

> I am the original fragrance of the earth, and I am the heat in fire. I am the life of all that lives, and I am the penances of all ascetics.

Even the sense of smell can help us reflect on an energy or aspect of God. Everything has some fragrance, smell, or emanation, and the earth itself has an original fragrance. This verse describes the *dharma* or essence of certain objects such as the heat of fire and the fragrance of the earth. The essential nature or purpose of all things always leads us back to the Lord.

> *bijam mam sarva-bhutanam*
> *viddhi partha sanatanam*
> *buddhir buddhimatam asmi*
> *tejas tejasvinam aham*
>
> O son of Prtha, know that I am the original seed of all existences, the intelligence of the intelligent, and the prowess of all powerful men.
> *Bhagavad-gita* 7.10

Throughout the world, we see great exhibitions of power and intelligence but for clarification, the scriptures tell us that Krishna is the one supreme source of all of these opulences: *krsnas tu bhagavan svayam*. God is the fountainhead of all incarnations, expansions, and entities. Throughout the creation, people constantly seek wealth, knowledge, beauty, renunciation, fame, and strength, but when they reach their goal, they soon find another person who has an even greater stock of these opulences. However, in spite of this competition, there is someone who has all of these qualities in full and who no one else can outperform. We can also appreciate the Godhead as the one who has the greatest opulences and qualities. His strength, fame, beauty, wealth, knowledge, and renunciation far surpass those of any other entity in existence.

As we reflect on certain aspects of the greatness of the creation, we can then relate those aspects to the ultimate Creator. When we see different *saktis* or energies, we should understand that they all come from the *saktiman* or the Original Energetic.

> *balam balavatam caham*
> *kama-raga-vivarjitam*
> *dharmaviruddho bhutesu*
> *kamo 'smi bharatarsabha*

> I am the strength of the strong, devoid of passion and desire. I am sex life which is not contrary to religious principles, O lord of the Bharatas [Arjuna].
> *Bhagavad-gita* 7.11

> *ye caiva sattvika bhava*
> *rajasas tamasas ca ye*
> *matta eveti tan viddhi*
> *na tv aham tesu te mayi*

> Know that all states of being—be they of goodness, passion or ignorance—are manifested by My energy. I am, in one sense, everything, but I am independent. I am not under the modes of material nature, for they, on the contrary, are within Me.
> *Bhagavad-gita* 7.12

The Lord clearly says that everything comes from Him; however, He still remains independent and outside of His own creation. This is the transcendental aspect of the Godhead.

Well Done, My Darling, Well Done

I would now like to share a meditation from my book, *The Beggar II*, entitled *Well Done, My Darling, Well Done*, in order to help us take this mindfulness much more to heart. We want to connect more with the transcendental so that the increasing degradation and duality in the material societies will not disturb us to the same extent. Mindfulness is a serious weapon that we want to share with you for healthy spiritual survival and even for material stability.

In this prayer, the individual endeavors to practice mindfulness and then receives great encouragement from the beloved. When people who we deeply care about act in beneficial ways, we want them to recognize their own achievements. We feel happy that they have enhanced their existence through their actions, which in turn helps us participate in their victory. If we do not care about a person, we may not even notice their outstanding behavior, and we feel hesitant to express any kind of appreciation. However, when we care, we feel happy that their actions will ultimately enhance their own well-being. We feel some satisfaction, knowing that their behavior will have a beneficial result.

> Today I practiced mindful breathing. As I inhaled, I imagined drawing in love, serenity, knowledge and bliss. As I exhaled, I imagined releasing lust, anger, fear and sadness. When I entered the temple and I looked at your picture, I saw you smile at me and say, "Well done, my darling, well done."

We inhale each day throughout the entire day. Consider the powerful level of mindfulness we can access if even the simple act of breathing functions as a stimulus to accelerate our consciousness and bring in more serenity, love, knowledge, and bliss. Furthermore, we can release all of the negativity that we often carry around such as sadness, fears, phobias, and anxieties. Although they come upon us at times, we can in fact release them. By accessing the love, serenity, knowledge, and bliss, we can simultaneously release the unhealthy emotions.

> Today when I went out, I practiced mindful walking. I walked for hours—I passed many people and saw many things. I sometimes had to avoid the danger of cars, dogs and obstacles on the road. Nevertheless, I felt that the sun was shining to infuse my body with dynamic energy, and that the birds were chirping just to cheer me on and encourage me toward my destination. Later on, when I returned to the temple, I looked at your picture and saw you smile at me and say: "Well done, my darling, well done!"

Just as we breathe everyday, we also walk. However, these days we might spend more time in the car or at our desks instead of walking, and even push buttons just to open the garage door. Hopefully we do occasionally take advantage of walking, especially during these mechanized times. When we do walk, we can turn it into a meditation to enhance the devotion. We can reflect on how the sun's rays rejuvenate the body and the consciousness, and the songs of the birds encourage us toward our destination. We can experience our environment in such a way that it becomes supportive to our devotion and our God consciousness.

> Today I practiced mindful talking. I was extremely careful not to say anything to offend anyone. I imagined that each word was showering another soul either with flower petals or with bricks. Devotional words are like flowers that will enhance another's well-being and celebrate that person's existence. Harsh or whimsical words are like assaults on others, as if stoning them with bricks. With each person I encountered, I only discussed devotional topics. Therefore, I was feeling constantly enlivened as I reflected on all of the glorious beings in my life. Later, when I returned to the temple, you smiled and again repeated: "Well done, my darling, well done."

We all talk so much but sometimes it simply turns into excessive speech and we lose a sense of meaning in our lives. Distracting conversations and gossip will then lead into superfluous actions. Sometimes we encounter people who do try to speak cautiously and sometimes we find others who simply want to bombard us with unnecessary conversations. We can find ways to elevate our discussions so that they do not drain our consciousness.

Consider the impact of a negative or positive conversation

in which a person subtly throws either bricks or throws nice flowers in order to glorify your existence. A person's harsh and whimsical words are like painful bricks, which cause wounds and unhealthy anxieties. As we speak, we should have that kind of mindfulness. Speaking sweetly, righteously, straightforwardly, and compassionately actually glorifies and celebrates the existence of another person. On the other hand, when we speak harshly or allow others to speak harshly to us, we involve ourselves in a battle and use these heavy bricks as our weapons.

If we care about someone, and we should care about everyone, we want to honor their presence by not attacking their existence with our harsh language. We want to have this mindfulness so that we will not offend others through our speech. Words are extremely powerful and have such a strong effect on the environment. We can use them as a means to encourage another person or as a weapon of destruction. Just imagine the powerful effect of speaking only healthy and compassionate words imbued with devotion. By celebrating and glorifying the existence of others, you will also feel stimulated by all of the wonderful people who you have honored and who are a part of your life. Such positive exchanges return back into your own consciousness and help you to be an even greater agent of divinity.

> Today I practiced mindful hearing. I reflected on how all conversation is a call to participate in certain activities or to accept certain mindsets. I chose to participate exclusively in devotional activities, and I only wanted to reflect on devotional topics. Thus, whenever

there were discussions that did not invite me to participate in devotional activity or reflection, I would simply excuse myself from the environment. I even went out of my way to seek the association of those who invited me to glorify the gurus, sadhus and the Divine Couple, and I consciously avoided the association of those who tried to entice me away from Their love and shelter. When I returned to the temple, I noticed your picture smiling as you said, "Well done, my darling, well done."

As we transition into this mindful absorption, we can harness the powers of the mind and remain in *samadhi* at practically every moment. We are constantly in control of our lives, which is a powerful attribute of warriors. In some of the subtler arts, the ability to control mind energy can determine the level of performance. First class athletes and people in general who have *sakti*, strength, and integrity do not allow the environment to distract them so easily; rather, they use the environment to enhance their particular efforts.

We practice mindful hearing so that we can focus at all times in order to minimize the distractions. Individuals who are weak in controlling their minds will surely have a poor intellect and will be slaves of their passions and senses. They will literally be at the mercy of the normative patterns of society. We do not necessarily need sophisticated formulas and rituals, but if we can remain constantly mindful, we will access many deeper experiences and adventures in our lives.

If we remain a part of sinful environments in which people

lack integrity and principle-centeredness, those negative environments will grossly and subtly influence the person because we do not exist on islands of our own. We are all products of heredity, environment, and the overt activities that form our experience. The environment even bombards us with so many subtle influences at any given moment. By hearing blasphemy, gossip, and harsh words, we internalize such language into our consciousness and these distractions will make it even more difficult to access divinity.

Conversation is actually an enticement and is never neutral. Any association involves some giving and receiving. Few people recognize this fact, which means that they simply get swept up by the environment without even understanding the detrimental effects. Whether the interactions are commercial, social, political, educational, or just between individuals, they are always invitations to participate in some type of exchange. Your actions and words invite others to interact with you in a certain way, and you accept their words as well.

> Today at the breakfast table, I practiced mindful eating. First, I thought of all my wonderful disciples who so conscientiously prepare foodstuffs for the pleasure of the Lord and myself. They always punctually prepare these meals in a clean, devotional mood and atmosphere. After carefully considering their service, I reflected on how the meal had been lovingly offered in prayer to the Supreme Lord, and how, later on the Lord's remnants were made available for others.

> As I chewed each morsel, I thought of how each preparation was now spiritually surcharged, and that by taking such foodstuff, my body was being fueled with spiritual nourishment. Then I thought of how each grain, each mouthful, was giving me the power to improve the quality and quantity of my meditation and service. After honoring this spiritual feast, I went into the temple, and there you were. Once again, your lips were curled in a smile, and you said to me, "Well done, my darling, well done."

As we develop more mental strength in all of our engagements, we will experience so many insights that we normally do not grasp. Mindfulness will allow us to increase the quality and sometimes even the quantity of our performance. We will not be as distracted by all the various types of incoherence that we normally internalize and imbibe. We will not allow such distractions to ultimately stagnate us. As we practice mindfulness, we will naturally feel grateful in spite of any of the circumstances in our environment. Gratitude will bring more blessings and help us appreciate those blessings much more.

A person can also get far more nourishment from foodstuff just by eating mindfully. The mentality in which we eat affects the entire body. In order to get the maximum benefit from a meal, we want to eat the right kinds of food, in the right mentality, in the right way, and in the right environment. Conversely, when people eat improper food in a hurry and in the wrong place, it will affect their consciousness and health.

The excessive fast food that people eat at improper places and times just bombards them. Considering these factors, it should not surprise us to see sicknesses such as ulcers and indigestion on the rise. On the other hand, we can spiritualize the whole process of eating through mindfulness and use it to enhance the devotion.

> Today I practiced mindful seeing. I reflected on how all things are composed of different energies of the Supreme Lord—that is, either His superior, marginal or separated energies. This allowed me to feel Lord Sri Krishna's presence constantly. Then I made a point of reflecting on the fact that everything I observed was coming from Krishna, and should be offered back to Him.
>
> Gradually, I recognized everything in creation as being a part of the Lord's universal form. Thus, things I would normally see as uninteresting, grotesque or frightening began to take on a far more meaningful appearance. Sights that ordinarily engendered lust or fear in me no longer bothered me. Instead of seeing them as objects for my enjoyment, I saw them all as aspects of the Divinity.
>
> With this new vision, I understood all captivating members of the opposite sex to be transformations of Krishna's

> beauty, and I no longer felt resentful of their radiance or inappropriately attracted to them. Soon, I adopted this attitude toward everything that spoke to my senses. Instead of getting agitated by trying to enjoy an experience, I saw each subject or environment that allured me as a display of Krishna's splendor. Later, when I returned to the temple and looked at your picture mindfully, I saw you beam an effulgent smile and nod, "Well done, my darling, well done."

When we have in our possession the property of another person, we then see ourselves as a caretaker. As caretakers, we want to care for the property in a way that would please the owner. Actually, by reflecting on God as the Ultimate Supreme Owner, we will put forth more of an effort to care in a way that would please Him.

However, instead of properly honoring the property of God, sometimes we want to own something in the environment and therefore we exploit, manipulate, and try to enjoy it in a sovereign way. Or we might use our philosophy to try to deny the beauty in the world but it is not healthy to constantly proclaim proprietorship or deny existence or beauty. Beauty does in fact exist but we can see it in an even more glorious way—as an aspect of the source of beauty. Then we can honor and appreciate it without the mindset of exploitation.

Sometimes people engage in devious behavior after seeing the improper actions of another person, which then disturbs or agitates them, causing them to lose their balance. However, we can examine our environment in a scrutinizing way in order to relate the objects in our surroundings to divinity. Then we will constantly speak divinely, hear topics that relate to divinity, and constantly see divinity around us. Consequently, we will respond to stimuli accordingly and even share and relate to others in that particular mood. For instance, if someone is fearful or very uptight, they will constantly codify the world around them according to their own particular mentality. Even their actions will result from that particular mindset. On the other hand, a person who is very loving will draw others into their mood because that mentality permeates throughout their thoughts and actions, and they then share that with others.

> Today I practiced mindful reading. As I perused different scriptures, I no longer read as if scanning a novel or ancient history, nor did I read as if studying mere philosophy or theology. As I read each chapter, I saw every section as a peephole into the spiritual realm. Then I would study the subject more closely and reflect on all the phenomenal activities taking place in the spiritual kingdom.

Most people read such material in a light mood and simply view it as ancient history. At best, they might see the scripture as some type of philosophical exposition. Mindfulness means going beyond philosophical speculation, religious cognition, mental gymnastics, and even just the rituals; it means accessing the deep spiritual essence present in all scriptures. Deep, mindful reflections far surpass mental or intellectual experiences. We will no longer read the scriptures as a novel or as a historical account that simply explores philosophical, epistemological, and cosmological considerations. It means that the scriptures will act as catalysts for rich experiences.

> All of a sudden, before I could stop myself, I began to weep incessantly, because I understood that no matter how much I pondered these writings, I was not yet qualified to interact with these great entities. Nor could I fully comprehend them, communicate with them or participate in their pastimes of adding to the Supreme Lord's pleasure.
>
> All this made me feel incredibly unfortunate as I pondered the irony of coming so close to the spiritual world, yet still remaining so far from its residents. I wept in agony, thinking: "Why have I been brought to the dinner table, but then not been allowed to eat? How could I be brought to the very tip of the window, but then only allowed to window shop? What is the value of all these mindful practices," I cried, "if I must continue my existence in this gross, material body?"

Sometimes in our spiritual growth we experience the dark nights of the soul or periods of acceleration in which certain events in our life entice us and make us want more and more.

We may begin to feel, "I have come this close, why can't I come closer?" This is the nature of true spiritual unfoldment. When you feel nourished, you want more, and when something happens in your life that excites you, you also want more and more of the same. You become more avid and eager for the next experience. On the other hand, when nothing happens, you lose faith, experience boredom, and begin to dabble in so many areas because that energy has to go somewhere. At this point, a person will remain superficial and not deeply delve into any area. Consequently, he or she will not have rich experiences.

Those who are having the deeper experiences are the most desperate because such experiences entice them to the point of wanting more and more. This is the nature of the soul, which is *sac-cid-ananda-vigraha* or full of knowledge, bliss, and eternality. Krishna states in the *Bhagavad-gita*:

>*apareyam itas tv anyam
>prakrtim viddhi me param
>jiva-bhutam maha-baho
>yayedam dharyate jagat*

>Besides these, O mighty-armed Arjuna, there is another, superior energy of Mine, which comprises the living entities who are exploiting the resources of this material, inferior nature.
>*Bhagavad-gita* 7.5

Although the Lord emanates so many separated features of His different energies, He tells us of His higher nature and its relationship to the *atma* or soul. The ultimate destination of the soul is in the spiritual kingdom. In this meditation, one is coming so close to the experience but still wants to experience so much more.

As the living entity unfolds unlimitedly, he or she does not have to leave this material world in order to experience transcendence. By practicing the proper spiritual technologies, we will begin to understand past, present, and future, and begin to have experiences beyond the gross material realm. We will begin to have experiences in connection with the spiritual dimensions, which will entice and stimulate the consciousness even more because such experiences are the natural activities of the soul. The soul, which has been in a dormant state, becomes so happy to connect with this stimulus. Due to this excitement, it wants more and more as it gradually regains its eternal happiness and experiences. One develops a genuine disgust for the material body that has its limits and restrictions, and is incarcerating the soul.

> I went to the temple and again looked at your picture. This time you were not smiling, but you were also crying, and this made me cry even more. Only now, to my incredible delight, you stepped right out of your picture and came up and gently embraced me. Then you looked compassionately into my eyes and spoke:
> "In your mindful breathing, walking, talking, hearing, eating and seeing, I was always with you. When we returned to the temple I smiled each time, knowing that you were shedding all the obstructions that have

bound you to the material plane. I was smiling also because I so greatly enjoy your association during these mindful meditations. You see, at these times we connect on a far deeper and more wonderful level."

Some people have perceptions of angels, archangels, and other subtle entities, but a person at a deep level of spiritual consciousness can have amazing experiences with the Deity, icon, or spiritual personality. Sometimes, certain powerful spiritual beings communicate through their voices, paraphernalia, and even through their pictures. For instance, in our temples and homes, we have pictures of *gurus* and saints, which go beyond merely aesthetic purposes. Such pictures actually emanate some of the presence of those spiritual entities. Anything connected with a highly spiritual entity will also emanate spirituality.

In this meditation, one enters back into the temple and gazes at the pictures of the great agents of the Lord and literally communicates with that particular presence. However, at this point, the presence not only communicates but actually steps out of the picture for more intense association, communication, and upliftment. This great divine presence then indicates that he always remains with the individual in his or her mindful state. If we can develop a proper mindful consciousness, we will go beyond theory and begin to experience the realities described in the great scriptures. Then, when we enter into a shrine, temple, church, mosque, or synagogue, we will experience more of the potency of that particular environment. If we maintain proper mindful absorption, we will even feel immediate reciprocation, blessings, and absorption when we talk to the pictures of the saint or *guru*.

> "So, my darling, there is no reason for your sadness. Don't become so easily discouraged. As long as you maintain your mindful platform, I am mindful of you! More importantly, when you learn to practice mindful sleeping, you will be able to fully connect with me, because then you will be able to understand one of the most sublime cosmic secrets: Throughout the day, while your body is active, you are actually in a deep slumber. It is while your body is at rest during the night that you are actually more awake.
>
> "At present, in your day-to-day affairs, you are almost fully asleep, but you are gradually waking up. So, my darling, please go into a very deep and mindful sleep—for in this state, we will be able to meet and communicate like never before."

Many insights come to people when they enter sleep. The average person sometimes spends over a third of his or her lifetime asleep but the saintly person does not take sleep as an ordinary affair. Sleep not only provides us with an opportunity to rejuvenate our bodies, but it can also give us a chance to connect with so many realms and engage in various aspects of service. Furthermore, the strength of our mindfulness in our waking state will determine the types of experiences that we will have in the dream state. Mindfulness can even allow us to connect with knowledge and blessings in the dream state that can help us function in the waking state. The spiritual masters can assist the disciples by connecting with them when their physical bodies are not so active. In this way, they can plant seeds, give warnings, give encouragement, and offer directions which will stimulate the individual in his or her waking state consciously as well as unconsciously.

> "I have so much to tell you, so much to show you, and even more to share with you. So wipe away your tears of sadness. In the near future, there will be time and reason for shedding an ocean of tears. But these will not be tears of pain. They will be tears of pure, ecstatic joy."
>
> With these words, you jumped back into your picture, only this time your smile was bigger than ever. When you spoke, you said, "Don't ever forget mindful sleeping, for it is through this mindful state that you will be awakened from your stupor of illusion and confusion. For now, just carry on with your mindfulness, and know that I am eagerly awaiting you, for yours has been a job well done, my darling, well done!"
>
> I stared for several minutes at your picture. Later that night, I heard your voice faintly repeating, "In all your

activities, always aim for mindfulness. And especially aim for mindful sleep."

Find the Miracles through Mindfulness

Many people ceaselessly complain and these days they do in fact have ample reasons to complain; nevertheless, they often put themselves in the consciousness of a victim, which means that they end up surrendering to stagnation and mundaneness instead of really making a difference in their lives. Unfortunately, they go through life feeling very dissatisfied, bored, disappointed, and anxious. When some people arrive at the end of their lives, they may look back and try to understand the purpose of it all. They will then think with disappointment, "I pursued fame, wealth, distinction, and adoration but most of the time I achieved nothing. The few times when I did fulfill my endless desires, I still did not feel any deep satisfaction. Now that I have reached the end of my life, what can I take with me other than emptiness?" Other people might wait for something to happen in their consciousness throughout their lives such as a miracle; however, the miracles are always with us, but we have to be more mindful in order to notice them.

By practicing mindful walking, breathing, seeing, hearing, eating, and sleeping, the material world gradually begins to take on the attributes of the spiritual world. Spiritual life is not just a sentimental idea that depends on emotionalism, faith, or sentimentality. It is a science that we can experience by applying the appropriate technologies to our lives. Mindfulness is one of those great weapons that allow us to focus and expediently attain the accessible treasures. Even when seemingly inauspicious things bombard us, if we maintain a proper level of mindfulness, we will constantly experience richer and more profound realizations. Then, whether we are in the waking state or in the sleeping state, we will have a wonderful chance to move closer towards liberation and our ultimate service, which is actually part of the eternality of the soul.

Questions and Answers

Question: I usually tend to take realizations that come to me in the morning as very serious. Yesterday an idea came to me and consequently I wrote a proposal that would benefit me financially as well as provide service for others. How do we know whether such thoughts come from a divine source or from a negative source? How can we specifically know the difference?

Answer: It is somewhat complex. For example, if we want to know which particular law to use in a specific case, a lawyer would have this level of sensitivity to the subject matter. He understands the rule of law in many different mitigating circumstances. If someone else wants to know which tablet to take for a particular ailment, the pharmacist would have a greater sense of clarity because he or she understands the disease, the symptoms, and the possible cures. We need to have some platform for evaluation whenever we want to obtain any type of knowledge.

Similarly, devotees constantly scrutinize the spiritual scriptures in order to clearly understand healthy behavior. We can also gain this understanding by looking closer at the effects of people's actions. After using these various platforms to make an evaluation, we then follow through with our actions. However, our own quality of perception and devotion will also determine how we codify situations. In very general terms, we see as favorable anything that brings more love and compassion, and enhances God consciousness. We categorize as unfavorable anything that disturbs the individual or the environment and brings on lower consciousness.

We can make this evaluation by asking ourselves the following question: If many people engaged in this particular behavior, would it bring about a greater good for a greater number of people, or would it disturb a greater number of people? If many people engage in a pious activity, it will of course concomitantly raise the level of consciousness of themselves and of others. To help make this evaluation, we can reflect on such statements as "Love your neighbor as yourself" or "Do unto others as you would have them do unto you." We can also ask ourselves before we act, "How would I feel if someone else did this to me?" If we feel comfortable to receive that treatment from someone else, then we carry it out with great eagerness. In some cases, it might involve some experimentation.

Early morning perceptions are quite interesting. As the day progresses, the general passions in the environment and in the modes gradually increase. People's bodies begin to wear down and the mental anxieties increase along with sound pollution, devious activities, assaults, and attacks. All of these negative influences just begin to infiltrate and affect consciousness. For this reason, when you go to different events, you might notice that the modes get heavier and heavier as the evening gets later. Arguments start and other problems might begin to unfold. You can take some of these points into consideration as you make your evaluation. The morning hours are important for any type of practices, especially prayer, meditation, chanting, and reading. If we engage in any of these activities in the morning, they will have more potency.

Question: I would like to comment on mindful walking. This week I had a particularly disturbing situation at work. While walking to my car after work, someone asked me, "How are you?" I replied, "Fine, how are you?" Then I passed another person who also started a conversation with me. By the time I reached my car, the negative incident at work was far in the back of my mind. If I had just gone straight home without any of these positive interactions, I would have been in an entirely different mindset. I do recommend walking if you can so that such positive things can happen to you.

Answer: If a person is in anxiety, even the cells in the body will tense up. Exercise and especially walking in pleasant places such as in parks or by water can help alleviate some of the tension. It elevates the consciousness even more. Furthermore, while walking, you can mindfully think with a sense of gratitude. When you do have a chance to meet people, you can try to share some love, care, and compassion. By doing this, you will see that it even comes back at you in the same way.

If you feel too uptight, just go to the park and show a little love to the flowers, trees, birds, squirrels, crickets, cats, or dogs. That will also come back to you. Sometimes people feel so disturbed that they do not even want to see anybody's face. If someone asks them, "Good day, how are you?" they might angrily snap back, "What do you mean by that? What is good about this day!?!" The person might even feel angered by the other person's smile and happiness. Sometimes we may just have to walk into the woods.

Question: Can we conclude from your lecture that if one is not mindful, one is actually forgetful and that this stage of forgetfulness actually initiated our material degradation?

Answer: Not only is this true but one who is not mindful is a "chump" because we are talking about war. The war is not just physical but also psychological, metaphysical, and spiritual. Someone who goes out onto the battlefield unmindfully is really in for trouble. It is very dangerous to deal with society along with all of the temptations, bombardments, and attacks without practicing mindfulness for one's health, survival, and spiritual growth. In general, people who have a sense of excellence and accomplishment in their lives learn more and more how to consciously and unconsciously focus and center themselves. They have some goals and visions that they want to reach. On the other hand, individuals who do not have a goal or a purpose in life will feel very miserable.

Question: Your remarks about conversations as enticements, invitations, and exchanges struck me because, in my work environment, I am frequently caught up in conversations that do not permit any discussion of spirituality. Not only do they discourage such conversation, they even frown upon this topic. I try to model some level of humility or patience and try to emanate good feelings, but while you spoke, I remembered a conversation that I got caught up in last week. Someone began to carry on about completely mundane activities and I simply could not just walk out or disappear. In that situation, does mindfulness mean to just remain clear in my own self about Krishna consciousness or are there any other ways to protect myself?

Answer: Mindfulness does not mean that we act rudely or harshly; rather, it means that we do not commit violence to others or allow others to commit violence to us. When people throw such harsh words at you or around you, they actually commit violence. When you accept it, you also engage in accepting that violence. When we see somebody who we love or care about engaging in violent and destructive activities, we also have the responsibility to try to help. For instance, if they are speaking harshly about another person, you can try to turn the conversation around by asking, "Yes, my dear, and how do you think we can help? What do you think we can do to make a difference?" In this way, you do not have to act rudely or condescendingly; rather, you have taken the interaction to another level.

You can also change the mood by sharing some nice qualities about the person. Everybody has some good qualities, and if we study them, we will discover such qualities. If we speak in this way, it will completely change the atmosphere. Of course, body language also has a big effect. If someone is speaking all types of nonsense and they see that they have your complete attention, they will want to give you more and more. However, if they can see that you really have no interest in the topic, you will be able to let them know in a friendly way that you do not want to participate any longer in the exchange.

We should be careful about how we use our time and how we interact with others because we have the duty to be our brother's and sister's keepers. We have the duty to love our neighbor as ourselves and act in ways that will constantly lead to the well-being of the other person. Actually, the behavior of most people now goes against their human and spiritual growth and it is very unfortunate if we do not try to help since we have the knowledge. For instance, in the work place, you will find that in many circles, people just tell offensive racial and gender jokes. If people are speaking in this harsh and negative tone, and they see that you are ready to hear, they will continue to share with more enthusiasm and might even approach you in a sexual or rude way. However, if they see that you will in no way accommodate such behavior, they will eventually stop after testing you. They will understand that you simply will not associate with them in that manner.

Otherwise, if you allow such interactions to begin in the first place, it will make it more difficult to stop later on because they will not understand your reasons when you suddenly back away from the regular exchanges. It will consequently create even more stagnation in the relationship. However, if they understand from the very beginning how you think and interact, they will not enter your space with gossip, deviation, drugs, or lies. If someone tries to tempt you with devious or degrading behavior, it also indicates that they do not think so highly of you. It means that they actually think you will participate in their deviation; however, you should not reinforce that mentality. By avoiding these interactions, you will be able to access more mindfulness which will then allow you to have a greater sense of well-being within your own life. You will be able to create that kind of force field around you.

People end up as products of nonsense and degradation without even realizing that they have a chance to make a difference. Due to their entrapment in this mechanized culture, they have little time to think. Material existence is based on what is functional, what is lucrative for rapid growth, and what will make money for the individual. Unfortunately, we simply turn into sophisticated monsters just trying to make the money. After acting as good monsters, it should not surprise us that we later feel so much anxiety. How do we then expect to suddenly come home and act with kindness and love towards our children, spouse, friends, and relatives? No, we will become whatever we practice most of the time. Considering that the average person spends an average of six to eight hours of their life at the job, it means that they spend almost half of their waking hours at the work place. Consequently, we have to especially practice this mindfulness at work because we do not just want someone else's negativity to constantly bombard us. Ultimately, we are accountable and responsible for our own lives.

Question: As we try to practice mindfulness, what role does the environment play? Last night we went to a *nama-hatta* program or a small spiritual support group. It was the second *nama-hatta* I have attended in several months. However, I could feel a distinct contrast between the two environments during these programs. The house last night was just filled with beautiful pictures and other wonderful opulences. When I went home, I had to apologize to my Deities because Srila Prabhupada has said that we should treat our house like a temple. The house last night really was a temple. Could you comment on this point?

Answer: Last night we had a program at the home of a very nice family—a husband, wife, and two daughters who are very spiritual. Their mood is so sweet that they are almost giddy. Sometimes people are so loving, kind, and happy about life that they are just giddy. Since they constantly glorify other people through their words and always try to serve and help, whenever you see them, you will always find them in this mood. Actually, this mood relates to their level of mindfulness. When you enter their house, it feels like a shrine due to the powerful spiritual energy associated with the environment. You can immediately understand how this family spends most of their time in their home. That type of environment also helps us understand why they act as they do.

Similarly, we can understand the nature of a businessperson just by looking at their desk or office. Some people use such insights for espionage as well. For instance, one mundane example involves high-level corporate espionage, which will continue to worsen because it sometimes can affect millions and billions of dollars. Some high-level companies who are into new markets have certain secrets, which means that other companies or agencies will even pay to find information. At one level, such spies often look for computer codes and passwords. Sometimes they can figure out a password by examining the information on a person's desk. For instance, a businessman might have a picture of his daughter on the desk, which means that he might use the nickname of his daughter as the password. Someone might try to guess several possible passwords through this method. Basically, a person's dominant environment will tell you a good deal about their priorities and consciousness.

In this family's house last night, every single room had beautiful pictures or Deities. The main room of the house, the living room, had five altars that just went from one wall to the next and five sets of Deities on the these altars. It was amazing. I inquired about their Deity service which they perform everyday. We can immediately understand that their public and private lives are similar. Since they have this powerful fuel and continuously imbibe higher spiritual consciousness in their home, when they go out, they just share all that they have internalized. However, we should also function according to our means. For instance, you might have a very demanding job and cannot maintain that level of Deity *puja*, or you might have many other services to perform for your spiritual organization as well. Each person might need to make certain adjustments according to their own lifestyle. However, from this example, we can understand that our home or office should also reflect the particular type of consciousness that we want to acquire.

In any place that I have a room, house, or temple, you will see that it has a certain mood. Devotees may laugh because I will even personally arrange the room when we move into a new place. I want to be careful about the energy that radiates in that room, and the effect that it has on visitors. I also want to be careful about those things that I must constantly experience in my own environment. I want to personally make these arrangements because I realize that the room will affect some of the things that I do when I leave that room. I want to expedite my ability to help people. More people are now finding out about feng shui which comes from a very deep spiritual connection. It is a Chinese practice in which structures or placements of objects are chosen to harmonize with the spiritual forces that inhabit them.[9]

In conclusion, breathing, speaking, walking, eating, seeing, and sleeping can all take on such deep potency and really enhance our spiritual life through the practice of mindfulness. However, the same activities can also lead to distraction so that we end up as products of mundaneness. Consequently, we will simply feel empty. We want to feel nourished inwardly and externally so that we can radiate that nourishment into our environment and function as love in action. We want people to feel uplifted and inspired by our association so that they will want to associate with us more. Then, they feel good about themselves and about life.

When someone carries an abundance of compassion and devotion, they automatically make you feel good about life. They encourage you to rise to higher levels of achievement; consequently, you will also want to be more loving. Love is contagious. Divinity and compassion are contagious but *maya*, anger, lust, greed, anxiety, fear, depression, and sin are also contagious. We have the choice to be either sufficiently mindful and connect with auspiciousness, or to be unmindful and allow the atmosphere to drain and disturb us. However, after the environment pulls us down and certain patterns have been established, we will then find it much more difficult to pick ourselves up again. At this point, the many subtle energies and forces simply bind us in their shackles. We want to make life easier and more joyful by accessing the deeper perspective and consciousness rather than struggle everyday with all of our activities.

As spiritual warriors, we use our divine weapons to cut away mundane attachments so that we can be profoundly mindful, making the mind our best friend. Try at least for one week to practice mindfulness in all of your activities and write down some of your realizations. You will be amazed—you may become addicted!

Chapter 6

The Perfect Escape

ksudrayusam nrnam anga
martyanam rtam icchatam
ihopahuto bhagavan
mrtyuh samitra-karmani

O Suta Gosvami, there are those amongst men who desire freedom from death and get eternal life. They escape the slaughtering process by calling the controller of death, Yamaraja.
Srimad-Bhagavatam 1.16.7

Escape from the Abode of Misery

The dream of every prisoner confined to a life of imprisonment is to make a perfect escape. As prisoners confined by the material body, we also want to escape from the material prison, which offers nothing but limitations and restrictions. We understand the nature of the material world from the *Bhagavad-gita*, which lucidly explains our miserable position:

> *a-brahma-bhuvanal lokah*
> *punar avartino 'rjuna*
> *mam upetya tu kaunteya*
> *punar janma na vidyate*

> From the highest planet in the material world down to the lowest, all are places of misery wherein repeated birth and death take place. But one who attains to My abode, O son of Kunti, never takes birth again.
> *Bhagavad-gita* 8.16

By understanding the depth of our imprisonment, how can we foolishly try to make ourselves comfortable in this realm? We live in a place of misery in which we find danger at every step: *padam padam yad vipadam na tesam*. Duality, pain, madness, and illusion inevitably affect each of us to varying degrees, as no one in this world is exempt from their jurisdiction. The material body is basically a bad bargain. The mere fact that we have a body means that we have turned our backs on Krishna's eternal pastimes. It means conflict and confusion no matter where we reside in these material universes, from the highest planets to the lowest.

Whether we have the highest and most opulent type of body in this world or live in the most degraded condition, the Lord tells us beyond a doubt that either place results in misery. He did not say that, in these places, we will only experience temporary setbacks, limited happiness, minimal pleasures, or small disturbances; He declares that they are all places of misery. There is a distinct difference between limitations and misery. A person subjected to various limitations can still experience some sort of stimulation, but the person submerged in an ocean of misery will not find any pleasure at all. The Lord informs us that whatever type of cell and prison suit we temporarily occupy, we should expect complete misery! Hopefully by understanding this basic truth, we can eventually rise above the entrapment by addressing the enemies of the mind.

The enemies such as lust, anger, depression, illusion, greed, and so on constantly beat us up, but should this surprise us? Krishna distinctly warns us that the material world will inevitably cause us all types of sufferings, but our craziness manifests when we try to escape by taking shelter of that very same enemy. If someone is harshly beating and exploiting you, how can you find relief by taking shelter of the source of your attack? Even though the thought of it sounds absurd, we sometimes do this everyday by taking shelter of those exact situations that cause us more pain. But people often make irrational choices while suffering in pain and agony. If we feel some disturbance in our spiritual life and try to solve the problem by taking some intoxications or turning to other sinful activities, we are actually taking shelter of the exact sin that caused our imprisonment in the first place. Rebelling against the laws of God is the foundation of our suffering, but many of us avoid this basic truth and still continue to wonder why we suffer from day to day.

Anxiety Versus Excitement

Why do some spiritualists feel so unhappy although engaged in devotional service in a devotional community? Why are we not experiencing what we often read about in the scriptures? Let us now analyze the difference between anxiety and excitement because it can help us answer these questions. From our previous discussion on enthusiasm, we can understand how it distinctly affects our ability to succeed in spiritual life and make that perfect escape. Therefore, let us understand enthusiasm along with its opposite—anxiety. In both cases, we see tremendous exertion of the mind as well as the body. Our emotions are either running intensely towards a goal or desperately trying to avoid a negative outcome. Although both emotions involve great intensity and focused energy, there is definitely a difference.

Anxiety is perpetuated by fear and excitement is perpetuated by hope. Both cases involve a type of anticipation, but one is negative and the other is positive. A person is either trying to avoid a certain outcome or is anticipating the future. Even when someone suffers from severe depression, we often see them running away from what they need the most. They are trying to escape from the fact that they have no excitement in their lives by shutting down emotionally or they try to escape the anxiety by narcotizing themselves through work, intoxication, or excessive sex life.

Furthermore, by focusing too much on what we want to avoid, we often draw that exact situation closer to ourselves. The mind does not always understand that we want to avoid a certain outcome; rather, it latches onto the object of our constant meditation. If we constantly dwell on the possible negative outcomes, we will create more of that in the future.

Therefore, by focusing with excitement on the positive, we can help create positive future experiences. Imagine putting fuel on a fire to create an even greater fire. Excitement or anxiety builds up tremendous energy that has to go somewhere. We either build up a mission and a vision that can lead to great empowerment, or we focus so much energy in running away which in turn creates that negative situation anyhow. In either case, an activity is being harnessed in some way, either negative or positive.

Introspect

Remember a time in which you felt intense anxiety and think of how it challenged not only your mind but your body as well in a serious way. Imagine an extreme case in which a vicious dog is chasing you down the street. You would feel extreme anxiety in your endeavor to avoid the attack. Compare that type of incident to a time in which you felt excited due to the anticipation of a pleasant event. In both cases, the mind goes through all kinds of gymnastics, which can even lead to a response by the physical body.

This is a significant issue as we look at the conception of escape and plan for our own escape. We want to examine our daily lives because we are always mad after some goal, either material or spiritual. We are either mad after sense gratification or we are mad after spiritual ecstasy. Think of your own ups and downs and the kind of madness involved in eagerness and euphoria. Think of the madness that ensues when we are captured by lust, frustration, gloom, and depression. Our consciousness becomes so lazy and morbid, sometimes even to the point of desiring death.

A Mission and A Vision

A perfect escape implies tremendous plotting, scheming, and planning. We sometimes hear of a person committing "the perfect crime," which indicates that they executed the act in such a precise way that they completely avoid detection. We want to have a clear vision and understand the mission. By focusing on the goal, we can gain some empowerment to act upon that vision. Wherever we see success, we will surely see a vision, which then leads to a mission. When we see failure, there is either a lack of vision or a lack of expertise and excitement to follow through.

When our material madness and anxiety decrease and we have more excitement about what we can experience, the same emotional buildup will go in a positive direction even though we are in this conditioned state. We will then harness the energy with a mission and a vision in terms of the goal. We realize our position as a prisoner stuck in a high or low position of wealth, poverty, beauty, sickness, knowledge, ignorance, etc. We are stuck and want to transcend. Krishna tells Arjuna to transcend and rise above all of the *gunas* or ropes of material nature:

> *trai-gunya-visaya veda*
> *nistrai-gunyo bhavarjuna*
> *nirdvandvo nitya-sattva-stho*
> *niryoga-ksema atmavan*

The Vedas deal mainly with the subject of the three modes of material nature. O Arjuna, become transcendental to these three modes. Be free from all dualities and from all anxieties for gain and

safety, and be established in the self.
Bhavagad-gita 2.45

Krishna does not even want us to get stuck in *sattva-guna* or the mode of goodness. Even in the more luxurious prison, the inmate still has limitations and misery.

Do we want to plan for an escape that leads to more imprisonment, or do we agitate the mind to plan for a real escape that will lead to transcendence? The atheists are surely making all kinds of plans for a more protracted imprisonment. But even if we are theistic, we will still remain stuck if we do not properly understand the science of transcendence. If we stay stuck for too long, it will make us madder for the opposite of what will really set us free. We will take more shelter of what put us into anxiety in the first place. This is the nature of *maya*. She attracts us with allurements that will imprison us longer and keep us under her control.

Keep in mind that Krishna explained how all the material planets and bodies, from the highest to the lowest, are places of misery. They do not just offer some slight discomfort, but complete misery. Misery is a heavy word. The material bodies and universes all offer different degrees and gradations of suffering. Why, we must ask, does the living entity do exactly that which will make it more difficult to escape? Why do we so frequently take shelter of those things that add to our complexities and our incarceration? Well, beloved, that is the craziness of material life and material culture. It imposes upon us and convinces us that we should try to enjoy that which will increase our suffering. We try again and again, only to repeatedly find out that the results are never quite what we expect. Furthermore, we know that for every deviation, there is a consequence and a chastisement. For this reason we say that there is no ultimate pleasure in the material world. There is *capala-sukha* or temporary stimulation and gratification, but there is no pleasure because such temporary gratifications just leave us miserable. How can it be pleasurable if, after every sense enjoyment, we get intense chastisement?

Find a Permanent Solution to the Misery

If Krishna tells us that this realm is a place of misery, surely He is encouraging us to go beyond and escape from the suffering. By remaining here and trying to make different arrangements, we will inevitably suffer from some expressions of misery. How do we get away? Most people are constantly trying to escape. Unfortunately, aspiring spiritualists often try to escape by taking shelter of *maya* in her other manifestations. If a person is bored or unfulfilled, he or she will have a tendency to escape into some type of *maya*, which could be smoking, drinking, illicit sex, or abominable food. *Maya* is trying every way to offer the body a chance to squeeze some taste and pleasure out of the misery. But Krishna has made it perfectly clear that misery is a part of the package. It is an inevitable part of the experience for each soul as it passes through the 8,400,000 different species of life. When the faith and *sukrti* or credits are not sufficient, we will end up taking shelter of various kinds of *maya*.

Spiritualists often have different bad habits that arise when they feel more of the misery always present in this world. They have their own idiosyncratic ways of escaping. However, this type of temporary escape will only bring more imprisonment. If a prisoner breaks additional rules within the prison, it will only increase his or her term. Instead of increasing their chances for freedom, it adds to their time in confinement. Of course, one may ask, "What can the person do? If the prisoner is in a miserable condition suffering from intense pain due to the enemies of the mind, naturally he or she will find some way to make a change." However, we must carefully select the type of relief that will benefit us in a long-term positive way.

Due to the fast-paced lifestyle that most people currently lead, they naturally turn to the quick fix. Obviously, the immediate response to pain is the search for quick relief. For instance, if we have a headache, naturally we want a pain pill. However, if a person has a tumor in their head, the pain pill with only address the headache—the symptom—without solving the issue permanently. Similarly, if we want a permanent solution to the misery, drinking a bottle of alcohol or taking some drugs will not ultimately help us; rather, it will only mitigate some of the symptoms. We might even think that a drug will increase our realization and insight, but such a cheap endeavor for instant spirituality will not help us develop an understanding of deep spiritual truths.

We might now wonder how to get out of this mentality of craving instant relief or instant spirituality. The deeper solutions to pain are rarely instant. In one sense, we need to shift our perspective on pain because the solution may not always be what we want it to be. It takes a certain amount of maturity for one to bypass the quick and artificial fix. It is often important for us to persevere with patience while pursuing a more thorough cure.

Follow a Genuine Plan of Escape

If we reflect on the rituals of any bona fide religion, we will see how they all fit into the plan for the ultimate perfect escape. The rituals of a Vaisnava such as chanting and glorifying the Lord help to actualize this escape. We are crying out to the Lord through His holy name: "Krishna, dear Supreme Lord, please get me out of here. Guide and protect me." We chant the Nrsmhadeva prayers for protection. We have the *darsana* of the Lord, praying for Him to allow us to really see Him, associate with Him, serve Him, and feed Him. These rituals can help us gradually move out of our miserable condition. The nine-fold process of devotional service is really a process of healthy escape. The more intensely and profoundly we involve ourselves by accepting the simple realities, the more we are preparing ourselves for the perfect escape.

For those trying to commit the perfect crime, they try to do it in such a way that the agents of incarceration remain unaware. It happens without their ability to check the activity. We want to make the perfect escape even with the enemies of the mind surrounding us and standing guard.

> To pursue the transcendental path is more or less to declare war on the illusory energy. Consequently, whenever a person tries to escape the clutches of the illusory energy, she tries to defeat the practitioner by various allurements. A conditioned soul is already allured by the modes of material energy, and there is every chance of being allured again, even while performing transcendental disciplines.
>
> *Bhagavad-gita* 6.37, purport

Even though *maya* constantly offers some illusion to confuse us and knock us off the royal path of *bhakti*, the attacks do not deter us. We find some way to avoid them. In order to escape, we must recognize the danger and the chances of failing. It is a reminder that we must maintain control in order to achieve success. While trying to move out of the misery, we must get help and make plans. We keep the goal in mind even while pretending to be a part of the normal environment.

Short-term goals and victories are necessary to give us more and more determination for the long-term achievements. If we don't have short-term successes, we will not even come close to ultimate success because it takes success to bring on powerful and eternal success. Something that seems far away from us will remain far away. It takes short-term victories to become victorious in the ultimate war—the spiritual war. It happens in increments and those increments gradually build up into *drdha-vrata* or strong determination and excitement. Excitement naturally happens as you have one accomplishment after another because you will feel excited about the next adventure and the next goal. Anxiety will lead to the exact opposite because you have been suffering with experiences of limitations and frustration; therefore, your negative anticipation will increase.

The mature spiritualists, while seemingly engaged in ordinary external activities, must be very internally fixed on a higher goal. The *acaryas* give the example of a woman who has a paramour. The person's heart and consciousness are focused solely on the lover even though she might be engaged in other activities. She does not want to attract the attention of other people who then will impose further restrictions; therefore, she performs the chores or household duties even more expertly to avoid raising suspicion in others. A devotee should devote him or herself to the perfect escape. *Maya* will offer all types of enticements, make us fearful, make us lusty, make us angry, or make us envious. *Maya* has so many weapons with which to expertly perform her attack. If one does not entice us, she will offer another or even many at the same time. She wants us to stay in prison. By occupying us with so many temporary allurements, we mistakenly think that we are getting closer to freedom while *maya* binds us more. We can go on like this for many, many lifetimes trying to escape through the wrong methods, but we cannot escape from the misery through artificial, cosmetic means.

The atheists also want to escape, but because they do not understand transcendence, they are just implicating themselves even more in the cycle of repeated birth and death. Therefore, some may end up inhabiting lower bodies in their next lifetime. Even spiritualists endeavoring to make an escape through the proper rituals and spiritual practices can become misguided by laziness, sinful reactions, doubts, and many more. Maybe his or her doubts have finally subsided, but the devotee just does not have a strong understanding of the process and lacks a strong resolve. In other cases, the devotee may understand the philosophy perfectly, but his or her quality of devotion is not sufficient to execute an escape. The enemies of the mind attack spiritualists in so many ways as they try to make it through the door.

In Judaism, a major tenet involves honoring the Sabbath—a time to help remind the individual about the goal. No one works on the Sabbath, which creates a more intense reminder that we are all meant for God. One minimizes the focus on the body and on the external permutations. In the Vaisnava tradition, we have Ekadasi and other important holy days in which we try to increase our chanting of the Lord's name, refrain from eating, or accept extra austerities. The point is to decrease our attachments and absorption in the physical realm so that we can intensify our focus on the spiritual goal. The holy *dhamas* or places of pilgrimage help remind us that we want to eternally remain in such places. The journey to a place of pilgrimage is also a time for rejuvenation. We temporarily achieve this victory or escape so that we can come closer to our ultimate victory of residing eternally in the spiritual kingdom. The *acaryas* inform us that a major tenet of *bhakti* involves this desire to reside in the holy *dhamas* because, even in the physical world, the *dhamas* are doors that help us connect more with the spiritual realm. They remind us of the activities that constantly unfold in the spiritual kingdom and give us some of the distinct culture of the eternal spiritual world.

The rituals that we do as Vaisnavas and in all religious traditions aim at taking us outside of the normative miseries and confinement. We understand that we are in this environment and in this miserable world, but it does not have to be eternal. We have the opportunity for freedom and escape. When we hear about the perfect escape, it also lets us know that most people don't escape; otherwise, it wouldn't be considered perfect. Most people are imprisoned and will remain in confinement indefinitely. Just as when we hear about the perfect crime, we realize that most criminals get caught. It is not so common for someone to execute the perfect crime. As we endeavor for escape, it is rare to find a person so focused and precise in their devotion, but it is possible. It is especially possible if we follow the guidance of those who have gone before us and have already freed themselves. They can help arrange for our own freedom.

Our Consciousness Creates Our Escape

When a prisoner plans his or her escape, the excitement about freedom escalates as the time nears. He or she makes so many plans in order to avoid detection. However, if the prisoner is too anxious, will he or she be successful? No, if they are too anxious and fearful about the negative, the fear itself could expose their intentions because they will raise suspicions. Or the anxiety could cause them to lose their dexterity when a difficult situation arises. When we are in too much pain, anxiety, gloom, or frustration, we can't possibly escape because we will fail to chant our rounds with sufficient intensity, cook with love, dress the Deities with sufficient love, or associate with other spiritualists with the necessary care and compassion. With excessive negative anxiety, we will lose our potency as spiritual warriors. By focusing that energy in a negative direction, we will distract ourselves. However, we cannot just stop the energy because inactivity will not lead us to success either. We want to put our energy into excitement, which will bring about short-term victories and long-term victories. Negative anxiety creates fear and stagnation, which will defeat a person before he or she even begins. In some cases, that defeatist mentality and lack of self-esteem will cripple a person to the point that he or she cannot function at all. Or it will create the exact situation that he or she wanted to avoid in the first place. Therefore, we must constantly absorb ourselves in transcendental literature and pastimes so that it will give us excitement and help us plan and execute the perfect escape.

Just knowing that freedom is attainable will increase our zeal tremendously. Some people have already escaped and we want to join them. It will increase our enthusiasm even more when we hear about their activities. We will want to join them to participate in the eternal, joyful pastimes. On the other hand, a person will inherently fail if he or she accepts the prison as a permanent residence and just continues to act according to the limitations. The whole idea of freedom will seem like a romantic fairytale. Since their experience is limited to the environment, they will not be able to even imagine another reality. While residing in these material bodies in these hellish material realms, we must continue to plan for escape. We do not want to keep doing the same things that have kept us in incarceration for many lifetimes.

The Need for Guidance

We might compare our position of confinement and our endeavor for escape to that of a battered woman or a slave in captivity. In the material world, volunteers have established centers to help battered women escape from their suffering. They often have to strategically plan with the help of other survivors along with various support systems so that they can discreetly leave. The woman needs a temporary place to stay, and, in some cases, she might even need to leave the city and change her name for her personal protection. Also, during the time of slavery in America, we saw the establishment of the Underground Railroad and safe houses to help free those in slavery. Those involved in the rescue efforts would make serious plans and often travel with the slaves to get them out of certain environments and states. They had to then bring them to a place in which they could stay and live permanently. In both of these cases, if the victim does not take proper shelter of their guides and protectors, they will have a problem in making the escape. However, if they lack faith or trust in their guides, they will not follow them with the same zeal.

The *acaryas* or teachers have the ability and proper knowledge to assist us, but they cannot help us if we remain stubbornly attached to our situation. If the battered woman is too fearful to make a change even though she has a chance and an alternative, she will remain imprisoned by her circumstances. However, if she has the proper excitement to make a change and escape from the torture of battery, that vision and excitement will help her attain the perfect escape. Both parties, the guides and the prisoners, have a responsibility to make this escape possible because the guides might be ready to assist, but the victim must be simultaneously ready to accept the help. Some people remain in an abusive relationship until they die. Sometimes it even ends more tragically if the husband kills the woman. Unfortunately, the woman sometimes has too much fear of the alternative. She might feel a little security in the relationship because of having a house and money and fears the alternative, which could mean no job, no home, no food, or no money. Or she might fear that the man will come after her. Of course, these are real issues that hinder the escape attempt.

Maya or illusion makes similar attacks when we try to run from her grasp. We feel it impossible to get rid of our bad habits. Maybe we don't want to even try because we do not think that we will be able to stop permanently. Once we stop, they will just attack and involve us again so we don't even want to make the initial endeavor. With this mentality, there is obviously no question of escape. Such people have already accepted that their state of imprisonment will continue. It is complex—the person doesn't escape because of intense anxiety, but the person does escape because of intense excitement. In both cases, a person is putting intense energy into their meditation. One who perfectly escapes anticipates victory and then visualizes the ultimate outcome.

Even when we engage in the activities meant for our escape, if we have too much anxiety during our services and spiritual activities, we will not benefit. At times, we might try to chant, pray, or meditate with so much negative anxiety that it is as if we didn't do it at all. Our minds were not present even though our bodies were engaged. If we hear a class and our minds are in so much anxiety, the message will not really penetrate into our consciousness. If we dress the Deities but feel so much anxiety, fear, lust, enviousness, and anger, the rejuvenating act of associating so closely with the Lord will not quite help us. The person who has spent too long in confinement will develop all kinds of dysfunctional patterns because confinement is unnatural. If we continue for too long without spiritual excitement, then we will once again start to develop all kinds of unhealthy patterns. As our anxiety increases, we will take shelter of that which will only make our problem worse. Unfortunately, we see it happening to us and around us as a part of the unhealthy spiritual journey.

On the Verge of Escape

The Fifth Canto of the *Srimad-Bhagavatam* describes Bharata Maharaja, an exalted king of Bharata-varsa, who had incredible opulence and facility to enjoy. He had so much fame that the entire planet was called Bharata-varsa in his honor. But, in spite of the opulence, he walked away from it all, understanding that from the highest material position to the lowest, all are places of misery. He renounced his entire kingdom in order to focus on a higher goal. He understood that even as a sophisticated prisoner, all his opulence, power, and wealth could not offer him any permanent satisfaction and would just increase the incarceration. His actions help us understand that we also should not put all our energy into something that will only increase our prison sentence.

Therefore, he left and went to Pulahasrama to perform austerities and worship the Lord. Due to his deep level of devotion, he began to exhibit symptoms of ecstasy, having attained the stage of *bhava*. Just as the battered woman knocks on the door of a shelter or a slave makes it to a safe house, Maharaja Bharata had made it to the door. However, a prisoner must still be careful after escaping since the guards will continue to search for him and try to reclaim him at all costs. Although he might have made the escape and has nicely settled into another situation, he must be even more conscientious so that his efforts are not in vain.

Many times people intensely involve themselves in this process of *bhakti*, but then become bewildered by offenses, lack of faith, and so on. Unfortunately, they come so close only to get recaptured. What happens when a prisoner escapes from prison but later gets recaptured? The person will experience even more misery than the initial term of imprisonment. When a person tries to escape from prison, the guards will monitor the individual much more closely. They have more security to make sure the person will not be able to make such a clever plan of escape again. Unfortunately, they came so close to the door that only a little more effort would have finalized their goal. When a devotee accelerates in spiritual life but then gets recaptured by *maya*, she will make it so much harder for the devotee to continue. *Maya* finds so many ways to debilitate and dismantle the person's devotion, faith, and support system. Now the individual is taking shelter of his or her imprisonment. From these factors, we can understand the madness and the danger.

When a battered woman finally gets away, she can make a total shift in her life, no longer fearing the moment when her husband will attack with violence. Similarly, the slave no longer has to worry about being misused, abused, and even killed. However, it takes great intensity to reach that goal, and failure to complete the escape once the mission has begun is even more dangerous. For the woman who does escape, she now feels so much compassion for those still in a state of suffering. The slave also feels such sadness to think of those still in bondage. Similarly, those personalities who have escaped from this realm or those eternally liberated souls feel intense compassion when they think of the souls still bound by the body. They feel even sadder to watch a person who has almost escaped fall once again into the shackles of *maya*. The person often becomes so much more demoralized after falling back into the trap. They might even lose their hope for future attempts.

While residing in the forest, Bharata Maharaja one day saw a pregnant deer drinking by the river. However, a roar of a lion frightened the deer so intensely that it immediately gave birth, crossed the river, and then died. Bharata Maharaja felt compassion for the baby who he rescued from the water out of compassion and then offered care. Maharaja, who previously put forth so many endeavors in his devotional practices, now put so much energy into the care of the little deer. Of course, his actions were ethical and pious, but still, we see the many ways that *maya* can disturb us. As Srila Visvanatha Cakravarti Thakura says in the *Madhurya-Kadambini*, *anarthas* or unwanted desires in the heart can arise due to past sins, offenses, devotional service, and also pious activities. *Maya* can distract us in so many ways because we can engage in devotional activities but serve with pride and greed. Bharata Maharaja had practically escaped from the material prison, but *maya* found the exact way to draw him away. At his level of devotion, he could not have been allured by intoxication, illicit sex, or any other more gross sinful activity, but he got distracted by a pious act. It does not mean that we shouldn't be pious, righteous, or ethical, but it means that when we have a mission to escape, we must focus on reaching the conclusion without allowing any distraction to hinder our progressive march.

Some people might get distracted from the devotional path when a seemingly good situation happens such as wealth or opulence. If someone on the path to escape is very sickly and their health is suddenly renewed, they may lose their intensity and ability to focus. Or an unmarried devotee might have been very focused on the escape mission, but, after they find a partner, they become distracted. Due to the relationship, they focus so much more on maintenance. Many allurements and distractions can disturb us if we are not careful. They do not have to, but they can. In this case, a small, helpless animal affected the heart of a compassionate *sadhu*. Look how *maya* came in disguise in such a discreet way. The deer distracted him to the point that he focused less on his original escape plan. As he focused more energy on caring for the deer, he focused less on his *sadhana* and devotion. Since he put so much energy into taking care of the deer, thinking about the deer, spending time with the deer, and embracing the deer, he gradually began to forget his original scheme just as a prisoner gets distracted by certain pleasantries, obligations, and associations that are not a part of liberation and freedom. These pastimes can help remind us that they happened in the past and can happen to us if we lower our guard.

One day the deer wandered off, and, due to his intense attachment, Bharata Maharaja began anxiously looking for him. In this state of anxiety, he fell down and died. Since he was thinking of the deer at the time of death, he got the body of a deer in his next birth. Whatever consciousness we have at the time of death, we will obtain a corresponding form in the next life. As stated in *Bhagavad-gita* 8.6:

> *yam yam vapi smaran bhavam*
> *tyajaty ante kalevaram*
> *tam tam evaiti kaunteya*
> *sada tad-bhava-bhavitah*
>
> Whatever state of being one remembers when he quits his body, O son of Kunti, that state he will attain without fail.

Bharata Maharaja, a great king who had renounced an entire kingdom became attached to an animal, consequently obtaining that type of body in his next birth. However, by the mercy of the Lord, he retained the memory of his previous lives even in that body of a deer. Thus he rekindled his focus on the goal. He left his mother deer and went once again to Pulahasrama.

After finishing the body of a deer, he took birth as the famous Jada Bharata. In this birth, he was again aware of his previous lives and aware of his tremendous failure. Even after giving up so much material wealth and leading a life of renunciation, he gave up his spiritual wealth as well. As Jada Bharata, he took the mission of escape so seriously that he acted deaf and dumb to avoid any more attachments. Thus people saw him as an imbecile, void of intelligence and ability. However, he was determined in that lifetime to achieve the perfect escape. One must be ready to make serious sacrifices in order to break out of incarceration. He did not even want the distraction of being known as a renunciate; therefore, he took the position of a dumb person so that no one would notice. He was in the world but not of it. In this way, *maya* could not destabilize or sabotage his escape plan.

His parents tried to give him proper training and he simply pretended to not understand. Finally, after his mother and father died, his stepmother and brothers abused him, treating him like an animal. Since he would not accept the normal life of a sense gratifier and the prison environment, they treated him horribly, letting him know that his life disgusted them. He planned and focused so expertly that they had no idea of his exalted position. He was now in the process of finalizing his escape. He learned so much from the previous allurements and setbacks that he would not make the same mistake again. He refused to allow negative anxiety and distractions to ruin his chance. Due to his internal excitement, other people could not bother him when they called him a fool, idiot, imbecile, and so on. It could not disturb him because he was internally surcharged with a mission and vision outside of this material paradigm.

One night, while guarding a patty field on the order of his stepbrothers, a group of dacoits took him away to offer in sacrifice to the Goddess Kali. Goddess Kali, an agent of Krishna, understood Jada Bharata to be a great personality rather than an imbecile. She could not bear the mistreatment of such an exalted devotee; therefore, when the dacoits raised the chopper to kill Jada Bharata, she came right out of the deity and killed the dacoits with that very same chopper. When we have the determination of devotees such as Jada Bharata, Krishna and His agents will help and protect us. However, we must make ourselves available to receive their protection. The more desperate we are, the more they will see our need for protection. However, we want to be desperate with spiritual excitement rather than anxiety. The more that we have material anxiety, *maya* will offer us many types of relief. She will find a way to infiltrate if we believe the she has something for us. We have already accepted that *maya* has nothing to offer us. All of these enemies of the mind are being guided especially by *ahankara* or false ego. As the false ego gradually diminishes, these enemies will have no opportunity to attack.

Later, the servants of King Rahugana ordered Jada Bharata to help carry the palanquin of the king, but he walked so carefully in order to avoid killing any ants that he disturbed the entire procession. He was far outside of what most people consider normal in this material world. Out of his intense compassion, he was concerned about the welfare of tiny little ants on the road. However, the palanquin would stop and go due to Jada Bharata's conscientiousness, and this angered the king who then chastised him with harsh insults. Of course, Jada Bharata remained focused and spoke very powerful philosophy to the king who could then appreciate that this seemingly dumb fool was not an ordinary servant. Keep in mind that even when he revealed himself, he did so at a time and place that would not distract him from his ultimate goal. He did not reveal himself to his parents or to the dacoits, but he chose to involve the king in his escape plan by speaking words that ultimately transformed his consciousness. We can relax at times, revealing our minds and hearts when we associate with those also ready to escape or those who have already escaped. As the king heard this tremendous philosophical discourse, he felt humbled and even offered his apologies and obeisances. Since he was a candidate to also escape from the prison, he did not cause any disturbance for Jada Bharata.

This pastime should not bewilder us, causing us to think that spiritual life is too difficult and that there are too many chances to fail. Even if we do think that way, look at the alternative. If we don't endeavor to escape, we understand what we can expect lifetime after lifetime—misery. Bharata Maharaja came so close but, due to his affection for a deer, he fell back into the normative patterns of the material world and of a prisoner. Yes, he experienced some excitement or temporary stimulation at having that little deer as his friend. He felt some comradeship and affiliation, which is how *maya* keeps us in the prison. She lets us feel a little happiness from time to time so that we simply look for the next temporary pleasure rather than the eternal escape. But Jada Bharata took extreme action to ensure that *maya* could not attack him again; thus he made the perfect escape.

Questions and Answers

Question: Why is it harder to make a second comeback after a failure? For instance, if an alcoholic quits drinking for several years, but then succumbs again to the addiction, why is it harder for him or her to quit after once again falling back into the habit?

Answer: It is definitely a fact that our activities become habits and ultimately our culture. When we have had a failure in our lives, it habituates us to more failure just as *sadacara* or good character creates more good character. By having failures, we gradually begin to accept ourselves as failures and even feel comfortable with that mindset. We no longer have a desire to excel nor do we feel excited about what we can experience. We instead put all of our energy into the anxiety of the failure.

This complicates the situation for those who first give up

drinking or smoking but then revert. For many people, it is like a death sentence because they have basically accepted that they will fail again. Failure leads to more failure. It makes the situation harder but not impossible. If they study their failure to understand how they ended up in that situation, they can make the necessary adjustments so that it will not happen again. By taking shelter of other people who can help them, they will also increase the probability of escape. As they humble themselves more, realizing how easy it is to fail, the failure can become a catalyst for success. Sometimes the greatest achievers originally had a terrible failure, but, due to their intense determination to get out of that situation, the failure actually acted as a catalyst to help them succeed. Then when they recognize a possible cause of the failure, they will stay far away. The recovering alcoholic will not go anywhere near a place that has alcohol. In this way, a person becomes successful.

Question: Religious institutions help to protect people from a good portion of the gross sinful activities, but we sometimes see that people might leave such institutions to return to their previous environments. However, sometimes we might encourage an aspiring spiritualist to go back to an environment because they might need certain experiences. There is a school of thought that claims it might help a person to experience a little *maya*. However, from your discussion, it sounds that such experiences could be quite dangerous and very risky.

Answer: After the inmate has left the immediate vicinity of the prison, the guide might give the individual a temporary spot to rest, but he will also warn the prisoner against unsafe and risky areas. The guide expertly understands the situation and provides the proper protection. It does not mean that, while escaping, the person has to keep running and running unnecessarily. The guide may allow the person to find a temporary place to recuperate but still within boundaries. However, the person must maintain their vision and excitement about the goal even though they need some time to rejuvenate. The guide gives shelter, but if the person starts to procrastinate, then the risk increases.

For instance, in terms of our *gurukuli* children, if we too strictly force them to focus on the goal, it might have the opposite effect. If they feel imposed upon by so many rules and regulations and feel unable to express themselves, at some point they will do just the opposite. At the same time, if they are just whimsically exposed to sense gratification, they will automatically get addicted and settle into the bad habits since they have been addicted in so many other lifetimes. It is very difficult because if you give them too much freedom, they will then get habituated. On the other hand, if you impose the rules on them too strictly, they will feel choked and make an unhealthy escape.

The Amish and the Mormons have established certain principles that are powerful for any spiritual community trying to be in the world but not of it. In terms of the Amish, approximately ninety percent of their children remain within the community even though, at they age of sixteen, they have the choice to stay or leave. By that time, they have experienced the environment along with its social and economic security, they understand the theology, and now have the opportunity to make a decision.

Although the Amish only educate their children to maybe an eighth grade level, they teach them so many technical skills that they can easily maintain themselves in a rural environment. When the child reaches sixteen and takes the opportunity to experience more of the world, the community will not shun them for their behavior. If they do decide to leave, their family will still welcome them back anytime that they decide to return. These practices seem to help maintain the purity of the community. However, if they choose to remain within community and formally join the church, they will be expected to follow the principles of the community and religion. For instance, if an adult seriously deviates from the principles, the family and community might shun them for a certain period of time. During this time, the community will not accept service from this person, but they can offer service if he or she is in need. This distinctly sends a message to the individual that they need to work on themselves to become a healthy member of community once again. It also makes it clear to others that the person is in a diseased state, and, in this way, the other people in the community will not also pick up the same disease.

Interestingly, most of the Amish children return not only because they have a choice, but also because they recognize something special about their own community. If the parents did not offer this freedom of choice, they might lose more of their children. Of course, some of the children get addicted to many of the allurements and don't return, even though most do. While the children go through this period of exposure to the so-called normal world, the parents and community are aware and can offer assistance at any time. They are ready to help based on the theology and the culture. Even if they get into different levels of deviation but later want to come back, the parents and community will make all arrangements to reclaim and help the person. There is power in that type of community. They understand that they cannot force a person to accept.

I have seen some communities in which the parents relentlessly force their children to act devotionally, but these children will surprise their parents one day when they become teenagers and run away from the process as quickly as possible. Some might even resent their upbringing. They will feel that they have been denied and abused due to that intense control and subjugation. On the other hand, I have seen communities in which the children have so much freedom that they are already absorbed in sense gratification at a young age and have accepted the mundane. I have the greatest respect for parents who are trying to raise children in spiritual environments. It is very difficult, but it is also the real test of how the philosophy is unfolding on a grand scale. The status of the children will show the real success of a community. The success will show in how the children can have guided and limited exposure that will not imprison them, but also simultaneously offer boundaries with loving guidance. However, even if the children have healthy guidance, most will probably reject it at certain points except in certain exceptional cases.

To just force children to follow strict rules and regulations will not work. It will cause so much curiosity that the child will hanker for freedom. But to just give freedom without the love that comes from monitoring will create a habitual sense gratifier. The person might have an unusual spiritual foundation, but will then accept the life of imprisonment as normal. Then, which route should a parent take? Is it worse to limit and restrict the child or lean towards excessive freedom? Each parent will have to make this choice for themselves, but I would focus more on the side of leniency. However, if we are lenient with the children, we should be even stricter with ourselves. If the children see healthy parents and strong members of the community, their examples will act as powerful catalysts for the children. It will help them remain within certain boundaries and prevent them from straying too far into deviation. Most important, we should focus on our own spirituality so that we will please the Lord; consequently, our own spiritual strength and credits will help compliment whatever the child lacks. Whatever way parents choose to raise their children, there is always a risk. Therefore, we should give more attention to our own spiritual growth because, as we grow individually, we naturally elevate the environment.

Question: We know that we should not be dysfunctional, insensitive, or impersonal but should try to properly maintain our material responsibilities. However, can't *maya* trick us as we try to become more materially responsible? It seems that *maya* can use this avenue to gradually allure us deeper and deeper into material entanglements.

Answer: We call this *prayasa* or overendeavoring for mundane things that are very difficult to attain, even within the devotional culture. This type of overendeavoring can be detrimental to our spiritual growth if we act as the proprietor and controller. On the other hand, we don't want to deny our responsibilities under the guise of renunciation. For instance, householders shouldn't deny their responsibilities to their children, wife, and families by hiding behind renunciation. This is unhealthy because householders should act as spiritual guides and take care of their families as a service to the Lord. Our renunciation means taking nice devotional care of the families and the facilities that Krishna makes available for us. True renunciation has never meant that a person just avoids work and responsibilities because of the difficulties. Such immature renunciation happens out of laziness or due to a lack of accountability. On the other hand, we don't want to involve ourselves so much in maintenance that we don't have time for quality *sadhana*. Therefore, we remind ourselves of *nirbandha-krsna-sambandhe yukta-vairagyam ucyate*: we want to accept things favorable for devotional service and reject anything that hinders our escape from this material world. When we make this evaluation, we need to honestly decide what is increasing our dedication to spiritual life and what is distracting us from our commitments. Is it causing us to feel comfortable in the prison house or is it increasing our eagerness to attain ultimate freedom?

The material world and its objects of enjoyment are designed to distract us. However, the scriptures explain how the same senses that can be stimulated for sense gratification can act as our source of liberation. The biggest problem is that the pseudo escape into sense gratification is always more accessible; therefore, laziness and a cheating propensity will always lead one to accept the temporary escape. But if we do fall into past failures, we want to use them as catalysts to more cleverly plan a perfect escape. We not only want to come to the door, but we want to knock and then enter into that abode of eternal freedom.

Chapter 7

Going Deeper by Pretending

*esa te 'bhihita sankhye
buddhir yoge tv imam srnu
buddhya yukto yaya partha
karma-bandham prahasyasi*

Thus far I have described this knowledge to you through analytical study. Now listen as I explain it in terms of working without fruitive results. O son of Prtha, when you act in such knowledge you can free yourself from the bondage of works.
   Bhagavad-gita 2.39

Devotional Service Requires Spiritual Acceleration

As spiritualists, we should always aspire to go deeper in our spiritual realizations, commitments, and understandings. Actually, if we do not go deeper and advance in spiritual life, we will confront many dangers on the path. Such dangers can manifest as a loss of enthusiasm, which can cause us to leave the process of devotional service. Even if we try to remain in the process, loss of enthusiasm can lead to stagnation or result in lack of faith. Not only will we remain stagnant, but we will also lose the ability to uplift anyone else. A spiritual warrior wants to have the potency to seriously help raise the level of consciousness on the planet. However, unless we grow by receiving properly, we will not be able to give very much. We will also begin to blame the environment and blame other people for our weaknesses. Furthermore, when a person does not grow sufficiently, they will feel incoherent and will normally find some reasons to justify their weak areas. This can lead to apathy because without enthusiasm, one will lose interest and zeal.

When we go through periods of stagnation, *maya* or illusion does not just stop her attacks and wait until we regain our strength. *Maya* does not decide to reduce her temptations because of our lack of preparation—she does just the opposite. *Maya* will try to attack us when we are the most vulnerable so that she can take advantage of our weaknesses. If we do not constantly move further away from her attacks and make spiritual advancement, she will gradually capture us, and we will lose our ability to be enthusiastic about the spiritual journey, experience its benefits, or even stay involved.

We actually do not have a choice—we can either advance

or fall into *maya's* tight embrace. As we look closely at these options, we will understand that advancement is not a luxury or an extracurricular aspect of the process. Devotional service requires spiritual acceleration and growth. Considering our current position in *maya's* camp, which constantly bombards us with the normative patterns of material culture, we will be captured or stagnated to various extents unless we simultaneously run away. If we do not go deeper, we could lose the chance to remain on the royal path of *bhakti*. Each person needs to constantly try to penetrate the layers or modes of material nature; counteract the enemies of the mind; and counteract the patterns of gross materialism, voidism, impersonalism, and sinful activities.

Those who reside in *sattvic*, mode of goodness rural communities can often understand the importance of advancement because such environments can bring out more of a person's qualities, overt as well as covert. In these environments, we have a great deal more time alone with our mind. Consequently, a rural or village environment can be very taxing, challenging, and assaulting, but at the same time very beneficial, because we cannot hide as much as we can in the passion of the city. There are also distinct dangers involved in not taking advantage of the process and going deeper in spiritual life. Most significantly, the mind will attack again and again. It actually becomes a good barometer to determine our level of spiritual acceleration. The mind's attacks are indicators that we must go deeper. It also provides a wonderful arena to more genuinely look at the contents of the mind.

This is an important topic because sometimes we serve mechanically or continue in our devotional service on the strength of our previous devotional credits. Then we forget the necessity, the beauty, and the adventure of having richer and richer experiences in our spiritual lives. In an evening *darsana* or small meeting on August 9, 1976 in Tehran, the great Vaisnava teacher, Srila Prabhupada said, "Rituals are meant for the neophytes who are given education to begin with. But if he's stuck up with rituals, does not make any further progress, then his progress is checked. You have to go, progress, more progress."[10] He speaks about rituals, which we must have, but rituals are only the externals and do not always involve a deep level of absorption. Rather, the rituals should function as an aid to help us access deeper levels of spiritual realization.

However, if we do make progress, we still need to take precautions because success can turn into our enemy by causing us to take certain aspects of our lives for granted. A spiritual success or even a material success can become our greatest enemy because we might begin to feel comfortable as a result, and instead of trying harder, we will continue to act according to our previous patterns. However, each situation now requires greater strength and intensity than the previous challenge. Similarly, previous failures can also lead to stagnation for the same reasons. A failure can demoralize us and even create fear within us, causing us to lose hope and faith in the possibilities that we can experience. We must constantly revisit the fact that spiritual life is a higher reality and it is available for everyone. We just have to follow the science in the proper way so we will have the experiences and realizations that are available.

We want to focus on the essence and push aside any superfluous or irrelevant obstacles so that we can dive for the nectar. Srila Prabhupada referred to this topic as "boiling the milk." In a letter to a disciple, he addresses the need to focus more on quality rather than quantity:

> Now we have got so many students and so many temples but I am fearful that if we expand too much in this way that we shall become weakened and gradually the whole thing will become lost. Just like milk. We may thin it more and more with water for cheating the customer, but in the end it will cease to be any longer milk. Better to boil the milk now very vigorously and make it thick and sweet, that is the best process. So let us concentrate on training our devotees very thoroughly in the knowledge of Krishna Consciousness from our books, from tapes, by discussing always, and in so many ways instruct them in the right propositions.[11]

In these letters, Srila Prabhupada emphasizes the importance of properly engaging devotees in their various services rather than just gathering many people in one place. He discusses the importance of quality so that the devotees can become more Krishna conscious and go deeper with a genuine experience.

Pretend

After establishing the importance of really delving into the devotional process and making proper advancement, we want to look at ways in which we can reach this goal. As a way to examine this topic more closely, I will now take this discussion to a rather unusual level—one of the best ways that we can go deeper is to **pretend**. At first, this may seem to go against every basic understanding that we usually have about devotional service as well as about all the instructions that we usually hear in self-help books and human potential workshops because they address the importance of authenticity. However, we first need to remind ourselves that all of our difficulties stem from pretending or more specifically, from **unhealthy pretending**. And every attempt to move through the mind's difficulties and reach certain achievements deals with healthy pretending. We can reflect on an example also given by Srila Prabhupada in which a person uses a thorn to get out a thorn stuck in the leg. A thorn is very small and often hard to get out after it lodges itself in the skin, but another thorn can help uproot the first one.

Nobody can really develop genuine authenticity without understanding his or her actual identity. Whatever we normally call authenticity usually deals with uncovering some layers of the illusion but it does not really deal with real authenticity. Being authentic ultimately relates to our real identity as spiritual entities who have an eternal identity, relationship, and service. Real authenticity means recognizing, accepting, and operating on the platform of *sac-cid-ananda-vigraha*. We know that we are *sat* or eternal, *cit* or full of knowledge, and *ananda* or full of bliss. Everything we do in these bodies lifetime after lifetime under the three modes of material nature occurs because of our pretense. We pretend that we are different from what we really are and we accept that false identity as our true selves.

When we experience fear, we allow the mind to focus in a specific direction of insecurity. We accept that emotion due to our forgetfulness of God because ultimately when God wants to protect someone, no one can harm him, and when the Lord wants to eliminate someone, nobody can protect him: *mare krsna rakhe ke, rakhe krsna mare ke*. If we are lonely, we are pretending that we do not have any association or reciprocation. We are actually never alone for there is the attentive indwelling presence of the Lord in everyone's heart. When we are experiencing any of the six enemies of the mind and their affiliates including lust, anger, greed, bewilderment, intoxication, envy, anxiety, fear, guilt, depression, and false ego, we are pretending that we are not loving entities. When we feel anger, we accept that we have a genuine reason to lose our stability. We then pretend to be out of control. However, in our eternal form or in our highest expression of our most authentic self, we never lose control. When we fall into states of bewilderment and illusion, we are pretending to be upset; therefore, our actions correspond because the mind has accepted.

Every negative mindset that causes unhealthy physical reactions has to do with our failure to accept our **real authentic identity** or in other words, with false pretense. Therefore, an important method to go deeper involves pretending or accepting the opposite of what we normally accept. The opposite of the negative tendencies we usually accept is our real identity. However, since we do not believe in our real identity, we pretend so that we can gradually accept the reality and become that essential reality. This means we "pretend" that the Supreme Lord always watches us because He does. We try to "pretend" that we are loved and appreciated in the most profound ways because we are. We can take this pretense a step further by acting in that spirit.

If someone walks into the room and you pretend that the person loves you entirely, it will have a powerful effect on the way you act towards him or her. Conversely, if someone enters and you categorize that person as your enemy, then you will pretend by acting in a negative way towards him or her, just as an enemy interacts with an enemy. If someone envies you and you accept that state of consciousness by pretending that they genuinely envy you, you ultimately overlook the fact that he or she is ultimately a pure person who has fallen into a state of temporary bewilderment. But if you pretend that the person is ultimately a pure agent of God, their actions and thoughts along with your own unhealthy thoughts will not distract you to the same extent. You will not allow the unhealthy pretense to hinder the unfoldment of your real identity as an agent of love who constantly embraces God at each moment.

In the purport to *Srimad-Bhagavatam* 11.2.42, we find:

> Just as a hungry materialistic man, upon seeing sumptuous food, immediately desires to put it in his mouth, an advanced devotee of Krishna, upon seeing a material object, immediately becomes eager to use it for the pleasure of Krishna. Without the spontaneous hunger to engage everything in the service of Krishna and to dive deeper and deeper into the ocean of love of Krishna, so-called realization of God or loose talk about so-called religious life is irrelevant to the actual experience of entering the kingdom of God.

Just as a hungry person desires sumptuous food, an aspiring servant of the Lord must have this insatiable desire to use everything in His service. We must look for the opportunities to satisfy the Lord with that same intensity. It all belongs to

Him so instead of pretending that everything belongs to us, we pretend that everything actually belongs to Krishna or God because it does. In this way, we counteract the negative things that we have acculturated through unhealthy actions and mindsets by pretending in a positive way.

Act According to Reality

We want to go on pretending in this way so that we can eventually become genuinely, profoundly authentic. As we function in this way, not just superficially but in a profound way, we begin to become authentic or *sac-cid-ananda-vigraha*. We begin to experience our real eternality, ultimate complete knowledge, and complete love and happiness. This may sound strange but try to imagine having millions and millions of people who are all pretending to be affectionate and loving towards each other. Imagine the power that would come out of such interactions. We are not just referring to a mental reflection but as they deeply pretend, they are thinking, speaking, and acting accordingly even though they have not yet fully attained the realization. It will have powerful results because it will soon become a reality.

Once a disciple asked the *guru* about the practice of offering obeisances. When a person offers obeisances, they humble themselves by prostrating their body and honoring the existence of Supersoul within another person. Considering this, the disciple asked if he should offer obeisances even if he does not feel these sentiments because it seems artificial or hypocritical. The *guru* responded by encouraging the devotee to continue paying obeisances because the right actions also help us to develop the right consciousness. In one sense, the *guru* encourages the devotee to pretend to have the greatest respect and appreciation for the other person and to act according to that type of mentality. The impact of the action will have an effect because the individual is in fact an agent of God and His part and parcel.

As we move about during the day, we can pretend that we are always in association with the Deity or ultimately in the spiritual realm engaged in all kinds of amazing relationships with the Lord. This is actually service within the mind, which will help us gradually come to the point of the full, ongoing experience. **This must be guided by the bona fide spiritual mentor and should not be taken for granted** but it involves preventing the mind from pretending in unhealthy ways. If we are still engaged in sinful activities, this kind of reflection is dangerous and prohibited. We want to recondition and realign the mind so that it will allow the actions to unfold the real nature of the experiences.

We want to look closer at this idea of using a thorn to take out another thorn. We have engaged in unhealthy pretending for so many lifetimes, which has created all of our mental problems and later physical problems. We have been such wonderful actors and even accepted our drama as the reality, but now we want to act based on the real drama. However, our pretense is so strong that we accept it as real, which means that just thinking differently will not change it quickly. We have to go deeper so that the reality becomes an essential part of our essence. What does a person do when they act and pretend? They do not just think about the part that they play but they actually act as if they have fully imbibed that identity. It is as if that identity fully possesses them.

We Have the Power to Make a Difference

We have the ability to accept or reject any of our thoughts although we often forget our capability to change our thought patterns. We should not neglect our ability to make a difference because we become our thoughts. When we think unhealthy thoughts, we pretend that we do not have any ability to make a difference. Due to our expert pretense, we have acted nicely in order to convince ourselves. As we focus more on the nature of our thoughts and moods, we will realize that they come and go like seasonal changes. However, we often pretend that moods will not go; therefore, we accept our current low ebb as the totality of our existence and identity. Consequently, we get caught in this mental creation. As we continue to think in negative or unhealthy ways, it creates moods. We should try to avoid doing an important activity in a low mood because it will have some negative influence on the outcome. When we are in a low mood, we are not at our best and not really authentic. A low mood indicates our absorption in unhealthy pretending.

We forget that everyone has their separate or individual *karma*. We also forget that everyone has their separate realities or perceptions, which we do not need to see as a problem. It is a part of the variegatedness of life and of Krishna ultimately arranging according to *karma*. Each person may not see or experience a situation in the same way. Sometimes it even creates a mental disturbance within us when we try to control and determine how people should perceive and act. We might expect them to all act and think according to our own codification and perception of the world.

Our feelings can act as a barometer because negative feelings indicate unhealthy pretending. When we find ourselves in a negative mindset, we must change the focus of our thoughts.

A low ebb indicates that we need to change what we are accepting and what we are pretending. As we reflect more on the present moment, we will realize that any past thoughts or actions are of the past. We have the present moment to decide what we want to accept because we have the **power to pretend**. Many issues that we deal with relate to misunderstanding our thoughts and minimizing our power to make a difference. If we feel powerless, we will continue acting in a powerless way. We misunderstand our moods because the material world means duality. Just as the seasons come and go and we dress and act according to those seasons, our moods will come and go and we will respond to those moods. However, we should understand that our authentic self goes far beyond a certain mood. Otherwise, we let the mood dominate and control us.

If we examine *karma* more closely, we will realize that each person has different influences acting upon him or her from the past and present. Of course, we understand that certain effects will continue to unfold in the future. It all relates to how we pretended in the past and how we are pretending in the present. If we especially focus on the present moment, we will realize that the past has gone and we can make choices for the future by recognizing that power within us. If we do not think that we have the ability to make a difference, we will not act. Then we will end up blaming the environment and finding reasons to suggest why we do not advance. Many people play that game, but they only cheat themselves.

Effort Versus Mercy

We now want to examine this distinction between destiny and freewill which has always puzzled philosophers and religionists. First we may wonder why *maya* and the pretense are so strong if the Supreme Personality of Godhead wants us back in the spiritual kingdom more than we want to come back. If we are originally spiritual entities in our eternal forms, why does it seem so difficult to think differently even when we want to make positive changes? The great Indian saint, Satyavrata Muni, had this same question which he presented to Matsya, an incarnation of Krishna, which appears in the Vedic text called the *Matsya Purana*.[12]

Matsya explains by using an example of a farmer who plants crops. He compares the endeavor to plant the crop to effort and compares the rain to fate. The farmer's effort to plant the crops is important but his effort is only one aspect because the rain depends on fate. Will the weather assist the crops in a healthy way? If the farmer does not plant, the crops will not grow whether the rain falls or not. Along with the effort to plant and the rain, the element of time also has a significant role. Even if the farmer plants and it rains, it still depends on time because the rain may come months after the farmer put the seeds into the ground. The rain may not come in time to nourish the seed properly. Matsya aligns this time factor with *karma* and with our experiences that control or dominate our life.

If we pretend in a negative sense, it relates to our free will in the moment and also from the past. It is connected to our destiny, which deals with time and *karma*. We can break this down in more detail. The Vaisnava saint, Srila Visvanatha Cakravarti Thakura, discussed *klesa* or distress in the *Madhurya-Kadambini* when he focuses on the different stages of negative karmic reactions. *Kuta* is the stage before the seed and *bijam* is the seed stage. *Aprarabdha* is the stage when the seed is not yet mature and *prarabdha* is the stage in which the seed is already mature. Basically, we have the seed or the *karma* and we have an environment in which the seed remains dormant. Then the seed becomes active due to the sin or the *karma* factor. Then we have the immature *karma* waiting just around the corner and then it manifests. In other words, we can have the unmanifested sin and distress and the manifested sin and distress. We reap the results of our *karma* much as the farmer harvests crops. Some crops have been harvested, while others are ripe but have not yet been gathered.

Another example can also help us understand effort and mercy. A man falls into a well and begins to scream for help. Through his own effort, he screams out and tries to draw attention. Then a person comes by the well and throws down a rope. The rope is the mercy. The person sees the rope and grabs on but the time factor determines whether he releases the rope or holds onto it because he might later become tired or discouraged and release the rope. Going deeper means that in spite of the *karma*, we grab the rope and keep holding on as the rescuer pulls us out of the well or, in other words, we keep holding on in our devotional activities as we go deeper and deeper.

Sometimes we have the tendency to make the effort and call out for the mercy but when someone throws down the rope, we might only hold on for a while. We do not feel comfortable with the way in which the rescuer is pulling us up. Then we lose faith or pretend that we have no help; consequently, we let go or stop bringing ourselves up. In such cases, we sometimes get dropped back down, or due to our loose grip, we stay in a stagnant position without knowing what to do. We may temporarily remain stagnant due to the tension and the precariousness of the environment, but after a while we will start sliding down. If we stop advancing and end up in a stagnant position, we will inevitably get pulled down. We do not have a choice. If the person stuck in the well does not continue to hold onto the rope and move upwards, then they will not be able to fully actualize the mercy of the help and the *karma* that brought them into that situation although they initially put forth the effort to call out.

We understand that the elements include effort, fate, and time. Then we must deal with *prarabdha* and *aprarabdha* reactions, which mean that sometimes we are strong and at other times we are weak. In other words, due to previous good *karma*, we may have positive thoughts and put forth effort, but in other cases, our thoughts and moods are unhealthy due to reactions from *karma* stemming from previous negative activities. Although we may feel strong at certain points, if we do not continue to go deeper, some reactions from past negative thoughts and activities will come and haunt us. In time, we get reactions from the past.

Sometimes when we struggle, we maintain our negative thinking, meaning that we will simply struggle more in the future. When we think positively during a struggle, we will experience beneficial change in our lives because the present thoughts will take us out of the challenge. Some healthy *karma* from the past will also come and will meet the good present thoughts. If we keep reminding ourselves of our real identity; maintain a healthy internal dialogue; and remain grateful and mindful, we will be able to move through such intervals in which we experience difficulties based on unhealthy thoughts or actions from the past. It could also stem from a temporary poor mood at that time. Conversely, we might have a period of growth and then begin to take things for granted. Later some of the unhealthy thoughts and actions from the past come to meet us. Although we may have been thinking positively, if we are not going deeper, such past influences will shift our mood. Basically, at any given time, there is effort along with grace and *karma*.

Desire and Deserve

The events that unfold in our life are a combination of what we desire and what we deserve. Everything that happens to every person stems from a combination of these two factors. What we desire relates to what we are pretending and how the Lord in the heart is reciprocating. What we deserve is also in connection with the Lord in the heart who is reciprocating based on our present, our past, and our thoughts for the future. It goes back to the same scene. The mind is accepting and rejecting. What we accept in the present and what we accepted in the past are producing our future.

For this reason, sometimes spiritualists are extremely compassionate and loving and sometimes they seem to be harsh or insensitive. Since they have so much faith in the Lord, they realize that He does not make any mistakes and everything has a purpose; therefore, they accept everything ultimately as God's mercy. They realize that Krishna gave us free will and always loves us; consequently, the way in which we use our free will determines our experiences. As we go deeper in our realizations and deeper in our consciousness, we will begin to realize that whatever happens to anyone of us depends on the aggregate of our desires along with what we deserve to experience for some reason.

It all relates to how we are pretending. If we allow the enemies of the mind to overcome us to the point that we feel powerless, we will get certain kinds of reciprocation and will continue to feed certain types of patterns. When we realize how expertly we pretend, it becomes less difficult to get free from the attacks of *maya*. Actually, we get out of the pretense by pretending differently; that is, **by using a thorn to get out a thorn**. Then gradually the real authentic personality and experience will come forth. If we do not pretend in a positive way, we will end up pretending ourselves into one suffering circumstance after another. Furthermore, we must take personal responsibility instead of finding fault with the environment. It is our fault because we have the ability to make choices at every moment.

Then a question of faith may arise. We do not come into this world with an empty slate; rather, the slate we have stems from the kind of pretending or the thoughts and actions from the past which have produced our current field of activities. However, if we continue to think that we are just products of the past and pretend that we are powerless, we will continue to have the same problems and even greater problems. When we accept the understanding that we can live for the present, we realize that we allow ourselves to accept or reject every thought that comes to us. We have the ability to make a difference because God loves us all the time, not just some of the time. He protects us all the time and arranges all of our experiences for our wellbeing. We are always in our original nature, which is eternal, full of knowledge, and full of bliss, but we have pretended that we are different due to our madness and craziness. Since we have pretended so expertly and created our own drama, we keep enacting Act I, Act II, Act III, or Act IV according to the stage that we have set.

Limitations of Materialistic Activities

We can compare the *karma* factor to a cow tied to a pole. A rope connects the distance between the pole and the cow and within that space, the cow can move. According to our *karma*, we have a certain situation, position, and constitution that we are currently experiencing. Much of our pretense has to do with the space or interval between the rope and the cow. How far can it go? We have free will but only a limited amount since we are still bound. When we talk about going deeper, we are referring to going beyond the distance of that rope.

All self-help, socialization, and materialistic activities at best can only go between the pole and the cow fully extended by the rope. This means that whatever a person does, he or she is still bound by fate and *karma*. For instance, someone may take a real estate course and become a multi-millionaire. Someone else may take that same course and fall into a state of bankruptcy. The techniques helped the person who had the positive *karma* to benefit from the available resources between the pole and the cow. The techniques can help us function in between that short space, but at the same time, we want to go beyond the confinements of the short rope. That distance can only be changed by *karma*-altering activities, which are devotional activities. Otherwise, we just remain products of the reciprocity of karmic reactions.

Effort can also confine a person because it can only produce limited results. The effort is still limited to the distance of the rope and continues to confine the prisoner. Although he still pretends to be a prisoner, he is making some small improvements in his incarcerated condition. He is pretending to be an improved prisoner. As we change *karma*, we change the length of the rope between the cow and pole or our entire condition of life.

We basically understand from Matsya that there is always predestination although there is also free will and the time factor. All of these influences constantly unfold at any given time and we have the ability to make alterations but not necessarily immediately. The *karma* or the sin will not go away immediately, but it definitely will not go away if we continue to pretend that the illusion is a reality and that it is impossible to transcend.

Healthy Pretending is the Authentic Activity

We must realize that we have acted our way into an unhealthy mindset due to our pretense; therefore, we can only get out by acting in the opposite way. However, healthy pretending is the authentic activity, which goes beyond just mechanical activities or mental reflections. Just as we have become obsessed with the negative activities, we want to become obsessed with the positive activities. Then that which seemed so difficult to overcome will become easier to transcend since we will have removed those false barriers.

For this reason, high-level devotees of the Lord have strong faith; they know the Lord is always present. They are even ready to go to the hellish planets because they are always with the Lord in consciousness. They know that their separation from Krishna or God is just an illusion. They realize you are in *maya* because you have allowed yourself to be in *maya* and you have the power to choose the good or bad. You feel anxious and bewildered because you have accepted the false as real and you think that you cannot escape. Therefore, you perpetuate the illusion and become your greatest enemy. You can only change when you realize that you are your own greatest enemy.

If we just keep looking at past experiences, at someone else's situation, or someone else's lack, we will miss the chance to use our own power. Therefore, the spiritual warriors have the duty to help people recognize their own resources and use them. Even if they do not like to hear the fact that they are responsible for their own situation and can make a difference, the spiritual warrior has the duty to tactfully help others. Our mind can be our greatest enemy or our greatest friend. If we pretend that it is our greatest enemy and act upon that categorization, it will be our enemy. However, if we harness it through the nine-fold process of devotional service, then the mind will become our greatest asset and we will act according to our real identity.

For instance, an extremely beautiful person might have convinced herself that she is ugly, but in order to change her false conception, she starts to pretend that she is beautiful. Although she is pretending to be beautiful, her mood is authentic because she is in fact beautiful. When she pretended to be ugly, all of her interactions within her environment as well as what she gave and received depended on that false conception of herself. However, other people are now encouraging her to pretend to be beautiful because she is in fact beautiful. Due to this mental shift, the way in which she codifies the world will completely change. It is a matter of pulling out a thorn with a thorn. Since we have thoroughly convinced ourselves of the illusion, it requires that same level of intensity to come to the realization of our real identity.

We can also change our *karma* through *prayascitta* or atonement. Although it falls into the category of *karma-kanda* or fruitive activities, it can also change *karma*. We all have certain things that we brought in from the past, which relates to fate. It is not permanent but it makes up part of our baggage. Consequently, by certain austerities in which we literally assault some of our baggage, we can change. Of course, the more direct and powerful way to change is through *bhakti-yoga* or devotional service. Austerities do make a difference because they burn up *karma*, but austerities take longer because they still deal with the externals. They do not always change the consciousness but sometimes they can gradually make a difference. However, as we go deeper in devotional service, we will see a change of consciousness, which then leads to a change in our words and actions.

When we refer to pretending, we are not referring to just visualizations or affirmations; rather, we are talking about pretending in a way that will help us genuinely access our real identity by becoming fully obsessed in a mindset. If we think that we are in Vrndavana or some other very holy environment and think that the people around us love us, we will gradually begin to own that within ourselves. We will also share that reality with others. But if we continue to think according to the duality by seeing people as friends and enemies, we will also receive more of that duality from others.

We do not mean that we should be artificial, because a distinction exists between artificiality and healthy pretending. Artificial people are just whimsical and have no integrity. We want to have such a strong desire for the reality that we will go beyond all orthodox and superficial conceptions of being authentic. We want to have such greed and hunger to experience the pure *bhakti* that we readily give everything back to God since we realize that everything belongs to Him in the first place. Every opportunity is a chance to either turn to God or to embrace death by taking another material body. If we continue with our unhealthy pretense, we will just meet death, and after that scene closes, we will get another stage to pretend again. This is the sum total of human and animal life; that is, the entity pretends and acts according to a certain costume and certain experiences. However, we want to get off that stage and really embrace our identities as eternal entities instead of just going through different dramas and nightmares. We do not just want to make adjustments in the middle of that nightmare but we want to get out of that situation forever.

Sincerity is Essential

One should always call on the names of God so that one may not fall down. When we chant or pray poorly and consider the *mantra* or prayers to be impotent, we are pretending that the *mantra* or prayer is not connecting us with the Lord and the spiritual world. We are pretending that we are just repeating another sound instead of capturing God's ear and connecting with the residents of the spiritual world. If you call someone on the telephone and pretend that they did not pick up the receiver on the other end, your conversation will be of an entirely different nature. However, if you call a person and pretend that they are on the other end, even though you do not hear them, you try to speak in a respectful way so that you can later discover that they were always on the line.

So much depends on the quality of praying and chanting. We should recognize what we are really doing when we call on the names of God. When we chant and pray, our minds and devotional activities all come to meet the *mantra* and prayer. If we have a hellish mentality and our activities have been whimsical, when we say the *mantra* or pray, we will lack sincerity although it has the potency to reveal everything to us. Ultimately, we are pretending that the *mantra* and prayer is not that powerful and will not have a significant effect. However, if we accept its potency, then we will **pick the thorn out with the thorn** and we will access its potency.

Many devotees just go through the motions when they chant, pray, and worship because they do it out of duty and some cannot even chant and pray at all because they lack the authenticity to realize that if you want the Lord, accept Him. If you do not want God, stop pretending and just call on Siva, Brahma, Durga, the policeman, the doctor, the merchant, *maya*,

Satan, or even your own name. If we are not accepting the Supreme Lord and we are pretending that He is not supremely powerful, we will continue to produce thoughts, moods, and feelings that correspond to that pretense and miss the chance today to connect with our Divine Lord.

Unless We Advance, We Will Fall Down

We cannot minimize the importance of going deeper because if we do not advance, we will fall down. **It is inevitable.** If we have not been going deeper in our spiritual lives, we are already falling. At some point, we will fall so low that we will not be able to pull ourselves up. We will fall to such an extent that we will not be able to transcend our craziness in this lifetime. By refusing to accept the possibilities, we will remain in our unhealthy pretense. We will make our soul enter into another body and accept another stage. We will feel that we need to have another stage in order to find fulfillment. Many people look for other material situations or alternatives because they do not use properly what they presently have. Some people have no other choice and will have to take another body. However, if they are not careful, they will have to act the same way in the next body, just as they have done in so many previous lifetimes.

For this reason, the Vedic text explains that at the end of Kali-yuga or this Age of Quarrel, the Lord descends to force change upon the remaining sinners and elevates them out of their bodies. The people will pretend to such an extent that in order to help them, some will simply have to leave their particular costumes or bodies because the particular caliber of that costume will not even allow them to operate so much on their own freedom. They have accepted their incarceration to such an extent that it becomes an integral part of their existence. Their only hope will be to force them out of their current existence so that they can pretend in a less negative way.

For this reason, the spiritual master intensely pushes us forward and also gives his love because this effort to push us to advance is also God's love. It helps us realize that each of us has the power. The Lord has given it to us. If we do not use it, we will end up constantly denying God's love and concern. Therefore, the spiritual master does not want to help us feel comfortable with our pretense. He does not want us to feel comfortable when we let go of the rope or ignore it completely after someone drops it down. If we scream for help and grab the rope, the time factor will come and help. However, once the rope gets thrown into the well, we must endeavor to hold on or, in other words, go deeper. If we do not hold on and fail to pull ourselves upward, after a while the pressure and tension will stagnate us. We may also begin to feel the anxiety of stagnation and then gradually release our grip and start going backwards in order to find some kind of relief. However, in each case, we have the position and the ability to make a difference.

Questions and Answers

Question: If we try to pretend in a healthy way by acting devotionally even though we may not have fully imbibed this feeling, we may have the tendency to try to convince other people that we have actually attained that level. Could you comment on this danger?

Answer: In that case, you are acting artificially because you are trying to elicit a certain response. We are talking about really acting or pretending to the point that you absorb yourself in the reality. It becomes you. Even though you do not yet have it permanently, you absorb yourself in the mood of having. Then it unfolds. We are not referring to artificial behavior in which you act in a certain way in order to draw out a specific mundane response or to manipulate and control someone else. We are discussing the importance of really existing in the moment so that we can fully become that in an ongoing way.

We can compare the situation to a person who has the chance to be a soldier. After accepting that position and wearing the uniform, he or she needs to somewhat pretend to be chivalrous, clean, and competent along with all the other good qualities that a soldier should possess. Even though the person might have the tendency to act whimsically due to his past conditioning, now he must pretend to be a respectful soldier and really absorb himself in that mood. He does not just want to ingratiate someone else by artificially showing a certain posture, but he really wants to convince himself by healthy pretense. After awhile he will convince himself and become a noble, chivalrous soldier.

Question: You said that whatever happens to us depends on what we desire and what we deserve. Do some things happen to us that are not really related to our desires or our personal *karma*?

Answer: The Supreme can give us a certain set of experiences that do not directly relate to our specific *karma* but to our general purpose. Due to our position and our *karma*, we might desire and deserve to be a teacher or facilitator for others, which means that we might need to have certain experiences connected with our purpose and not with our specific *karma*. Such experiences will ultimately help us empathize or help others who do have this specific *karma*.

Sometimes certain things manifest that do not directly relate to a person's own particular activity but to their quality. If a person has the quality to be a facilitator, they will go through certain experiences that will prepare them for what they have to do in the future. However, all of this is related to their quality, which depends on what they deserve and what they desire. Since we are cheaters, and in many ways angry with God, the living entity as well as the pseudo-spiritualist has the tendency to either directly or indirectly place the Lord at fault. This happens when a person must undergo an experience that they feel did not develop from their quality, thoughts, or actions. As a result, they basically feel that God cheated them or made a mistake.

Keep in mind that the Supreme Personality of Godhead makes arrangements in disguise. For instance, a person may be born in a family with a very obnoxious mother although the person might have very auspicious qualities. In the case of Prahlada Maharaja, a very young and pure boy in Vedic history whose father was a demon, his specific actions did not bring him that father but his quality brought him that situation so that he could show the world the result of purity in spite of any calamities in the external environment. A mother may have a blind child who she must carefully assist every day but it does not mean that some bad reaction brought that child to the mother. Her own qualities and desires along with what she deserves allows her to have a child that will help her develop more empathy and concern for the needs of others. The lessons do not necessarily come in the form that we expect but they come because some aspect of our character or desires has elicited a certain situation.

Karma is very exact and the Supreme is the most exact. For this reason, we refer to Him as the *summum bonum* and the Absolute Truth. When people see their problems as insurmountable, it means that they really lack faith in God. When people feel that they should not have to experience a specific problem, they actually blame the Lord or consider Him to be unfair. For this reason, we look at the lives of all the great devotees from all the different *varnas* and *asramas* or social and religious orders who underwent poverty, wealth, sickness, and health because they always maintained their love and faith in God. They always remain consistent in honoring God in spite of whatever situation He gives to them. They are always full of gratitude and profoundly mindful.

A person must genuinely have this depth in order to return to the spiritual world. Until we really go deeper, we will continue to suffer because we will feel the pain and tension in our arms from holding onto the rope. When the pain increases, we will either drop it or slide down. We might even begin to curse the people at the top, blaming them for our fall. Or we will lose enthusiasm, begin to fault-find, and lose faith. All of these negative mindsets will develop due to our cheating propensity that also relates to our own choices and unhealthy pretending. We complicate things that are so simple and essential—this is the nature of *maya*. She puts so many blocks between us and Krishna's dynamic love. The whole aspect of *samsara* or repeated birth and death emerges as we accept more superfluous things that minimize calling on the Lord and receiving His message.

Question: It seems that the difference between healthy and unhealthy pretending has to do with faith.

Answer: Yes, it depends on who and what we have faith in along with the quality of that faith. Everyone has faith in something or someone. Faith can be influenced by the modes of ignorance, passion, or goodness, but faith can also be affiliated with transcendence. Who and what our faith is associated with will determine our experiences, realizations, and degree of spiritual acceleration. Weak and poor faith alignments bring unhealthy pretending; strong, mature faith alignments bring healthy pretending from productive visualizations, anticipations, and accelerations.

Question: You discussed the importance of identifying with our quality as *sac-cid-ananda-vigraha* and referred to this in connection with *mana-seva*. You then described the importance of receiving guidance through this period. Can you explain more on this point?

Answer: In the *Harinama Cintamani*, a powerful book on the efficacy of chanting the holy name of the Lord, the author Haridasa Thakura discusses how the spiritual master guides the disciple into awareness of his or her original *svarupa* or eternal existence in relation to Krishna in the spiritual world. Although the disciple still has a physical body, there are some instructions and spiritual sciences involving the mind that allow him to gradually uncover his original identity in the spiritual world. It also discusses how the spiritual master somewhat presents a possible situation just as a tailor fixes a suit. However, the receiver of the suit still has the ability to accept it as it is or request some alterations. This is all a part of a very esoteric science. It is a part of our line as Gaudiya Vaisnavas but is not to be approached superficially or by one who is still sinful.

Our immediate teacher did not place so much emphasis on

this topic because of the many *sahajiyas* or deviant spiritualists at that time. They were trying to enter into this science without the proper *adhikara* or qualifications, and therefore they were being artificial rather than pretending transcendentally or spiritually focusing the mind. Such activity genuinely practiced is aligned with the activity of going deeper with mind quality and culture. Although the body remains involved in the external world, the mind is going deeper and breaking through the modes of material nature so that we are no longer confined to the experiences in the immediate environment.

Question: Thank you very much for discussing this topic. At one point, you started to say how to go deeper. Are you saying that in order to go deeper, such practices as improved praying, chanting, worshiping, and following the orders of the spiritual master are of great importance?

Answer: Yes, we must engage in all of these aspects of *sadhana-bhakti* or the devotional culture but there must be *laulya* or spiritual greed. We are really trying to focus on the importance of greed. Recognizing the possibilities as well as understanding the nature of the enemies of the mind helps us intensify the spiritual greed. As the greed intensifies, we will have the ability to make a shift away from being victims of previous *karma* and from the crazy patterns in the mind. Many of the problems within our minds develop because we have accepted mediocrity and failure. We will be able to accept success and achievement much more easily when we accept the true nature of our real identity. We are simply blocking ourselves from receiving all that is available.

Accepting our real identity is an orientation into the recognition of the power invested within us. It is an orientation into the recognition of the love that surrounds us all the time although we constantly deny it. We have made many constructs by accepting unhealthy mindsets such as chronic anxiety, phobias, grief, posttraumatic stress, obsessive compulsion, fear, depression, anger, lust, enviousness, and all types of illusions. However, since we had the choice to accept them, we can also make the decision to reject them. We have used our free will to accept and fully identify with unhealthy constructs without realizing that we have the ability to also release and reject them. We can have the enthusiasm and greed to remove the negative and embrace that which will properly stimulate and rejuvenate us.

However, if we continue to consider change impossible, represented by our unhealthy internal dialogue, we will go on artificially and maybe even talk about the authentic, but we will continue in the same life space. We will hold onto the rope for a period of time, but if we do not understand that we can get out of the well by pulling upward, the restrictions and limitations of the well will just capture us. We will gradually accept that unnatural situation as our permanent reality. Once we let go of the rope, we either lose our chance for liberation or we get so captured by our failure that we lose enthusiasm, blaspheme, offend others, or scapegoat due to our misery. In many cases, it means another lifetime and body in which we will get another field of activity. We will have another chance to grab the rope but hopefully this time we will hold on tight.

Question: Are you saying that we should basically accept the possibility and desire for full God consciousness to happen in our present life because then that will occur?

Answer: Absolutely. Yes, accept the available reality and be spiritually greedy! If we do not accept the realities or the possibilities, how can we endeavor to reach that goal? If we do not accept it, it indicates that our internal dialogue just revolves around impoverishment, defeat, and limitations. We will simply think that the Lord does not treat us fairly. Even though we are artificially speaking differently, we are not really pretending or accepting the different thoughts.

Question: Does Krishna ever take someone's free will away? The great souls pray to Krishna that He will never let them forget Him but it seems that their own free will lets them engage in service.

Answer: If I am driving a car but then stop and give you the keys, I have allowed you to control my destiny at that point to a certain extent. I have given that power over to you. Of course, Krishna is the best driver so we can offer our free will back to Him and let Him drive. We do not really give up our freedom although we use that terminology when we pray, "Take back my free will, dear Lord." Actually, it really means that we will use our free will to the maximum. With our full energy and consciousness, we will use that freedom and give it to the Lord. We will give the keys to the Lord so that He can drive because we understand His exceptional ability to drive the car. As a result, we will arrive at the destination faster and more safely because He drives far better than anyone else.

However, another person might not hand the keys over because they want to be the determining factor in their own life and destiny. Although the person does not really have the skills to drive efficiently, he or she wants to drive. He may think that he has a better position since he has control of the wheel but he actually limits himself due to his own lack of expertise and dexterity. Therefore, the person who wants the Lord to drive acts as the Lord's puppet.

Remember that of all the *angas* or limbs of *bhakti*, the *svarupa-laksana* or the defining quality of a Vaisnava, which is full dependence on the Lord, is the most important. Ultimately, in our deepest state of realization, everything depends on how much we understand this basic truth. Conversely, all of our *maya* depends on our distance from this realization. If God does have all of these supreme qualities, then we have the perfect formula. If the Lord is not ultimately loving and concerned about our welfare to the highest extent, then the situation is different, but if He is fully benevolent, we will unfold to the degree that we depend on Him. If He is genuine about His promise to reward us according to our level of surrender, we will achieve the full results according to our level of surrender.

The choices that we make and the desires that we have will produce what we deserve. Basically, the greatest expression of freedom is to offer our free will to the Lord. We have that personal choice. All we are really saying is that we are tired of getting in the way. Since we have had enough, we believe in the *siddhanta* or spiritual conclusion and are ready to dive deeper. In order to do this, we must accept and have faith in God's power, compassion, and love for us.

Question: Can you explain the difference between stagnation and steadiness? In terms of driving, you cannot always be in the same gear, especially when you are going uphill.

Answer: Not only can we not progress if we remain in the same gear, it is inevitable that we will have to change to a different gear. As long as we are in the material world, we will experience duality. Until we are completely pure, the duality will come and affect us. Krishna says that one who is dear to Him is unaffected by happiness and distress. He did not say that the person will not experience duality in the environment or that it will not assault him or her. Even though we use that term often, steadiness is dangerous. A person cannot be steady without making proper advancement. Steadiness means that you are pulling away from the illusion but not with a tremendous force because you are pulling away just enough to avoid getting pulled into the illusion. We want to go beyond steadiness, which is mediocre, because we want to advance by big increments, moving forward at great distances.

For instance, if I am pulling you, your ability to remain steady means that you must use an equal amount of strength to remain in your position. I will not be able to pull you towards me if you are using a sufficient amount of strength to pull in your direction. You will remain situated. However, if you simply try to remain steady, I will be able to perhaps gradually pull you in. Similarly, if we are advancing in just a small way, we are actually steady; that is, still too close to failure or being captured by sin. We want to advance seriously so that we can really move far away from the sins and illusions, the opposite pulling forces.

This point somewhat summarizes the essence of this discussion. If we are not advancing, we are falling. If we do not have serious faith, then there are different ways that we are consciously or unconsciously being pulled over to *maya*, often blaming the Supreme Godhead in the process. If we do not sufficiently accept God as the ultimate controller and well-wisher, we are not accepting our own influence and power over the things that happen to us. We are unhealthily pretending to be powerless.

Question: A hypothetical question came to mind during your class. A devotee may go on pretending with his thoughts and actions but then the three modes of nature come along and overpower the devotee. The devotee feels impelled to act in such a way that he has a fall down and then no longer feels like a good devotee. He or she does not feel like acting properly any more and consequently, slips backwards for a period of time. Can you give some advice to a devotee who finds him or herself in this situation?

Answer: For this reason, we stated that both success and failure can lead to stagnation. After a success, we may relax and just continue to function in the same way without going deeper or preparing sufficiently for the next battle or challenge. When we have a failure, we may begin to think of ourselves as failures instead of just recognizing that we made a mistake. Therefore, we want to try to live in the present moment and look closer at our internal identity. We should expect that *karma* and the modes will bother us in different ways but the problem arises when we accept this duality to be the only reality. For instance, we might accept that winter is a permanent condition instead of a transitory aspect of the change of seasons. Actually, we realize that winter with all of its cold weather and snow is a reality but a temporary reality. By accepting this fact, we will become even more excited when summer comes. Later, we will even begin to plan for the winter ahead of time so that we can minimize its difficulties.

Therefore, even when we start pretending in an unhealthy way and allow the enemies of the mind to capture us, they will not devour us because we will understand that we just lost control. Then we will pull ourselves back on track. We understand that we just forgot our real identity and instead reverted to some previous patterns. However, those patterns are not our real identity and we can move away from them. There are times when we will have setbacks or some heavy *karma* from the past will just sweep us away. Our unmanifested *karma* will just fall on us, which is part of the fate at that time. However, it is not fate to its entirety and it is not our permanent condition; rather, it is only the fate that we experience at that time. If we accept a higher reality differently in the present, the future will also change.

For this reason, I shared the verse that explains how the difficulties do not necessarily change right away but nevertheless one should go on with faith and determination.

> My dear Lord, one who earnestly waits for You to bestow Your causeless mercy upon him, all the while patiently suffering the reactions of his past misdeeds and offering You respectful obeisances with his heart, words and body, is surely eligible for liberation, for it has become his rightful claim.
> *Srimad-Bhagavatam* 10.14.8

Just because someone tries to connect properly to the system, it does not mean that everything will immediately go smoothly. It can as in Dhruva Maharaja's case happen quickly but that is rare and exceptional. Regardless, a person should go on, knowing that it becomes his or her rightful claim to inherit the Kingdom of God. This prayer emphasizes the fact that sometimes we may be acting in the right way but the results have not manifested yet. However, if we have the faith and understanding, it allows us to remain fixed until things begin to shift.

Amazingly, it always returns to the aspect of faith because without sufficient faith, when you fall into a lower ebb, you will give in to the temptations. Although you may have the proper knowledge, without sufficient faith, you may not be able to act upon it or the mind will try to find ways to try to deny the obvious realities. Faith is also a part of previous *karma* and present desires, which will determine the extent to which the Lord facilitates us because faith comes so much from the Lord in the heart. Faith makes the distinction between the advanced, intermediate, or neophyte devotee. It all depends on the quality of faith. It determines how much we pretend in a negative sense or pretend in a genuine way. It all relates to faith, which determines the degree to which we let the Supreme Lord come through. He has already arranged for our rescue when we fall into the well but most ignore His mercy or only accept it temporarily or superficially. He is the best driver and will bring us home nicely, but if we keep pretending to be the best, we will settle for less.

Epilogue

If we pretend in a negative sense by accepting and holding onto the enemies of the mind and their affiliates, we will continue to put ourselves in suffering conditions day after day; week after week; month after month; year after year; decade after decade; and, yes, even lifetime after lifetime. The mental suffering of people on this planet is increasing daily which is manifesting in the yearly rise of mental illness and especially depression. Millions of people are wounded and are becoming casualties.

The battlefield of consciousness has always been the most serious area of conflict. The mind is so often our greatest enemy, but we must turn it into our great friend; otherwise, it will eventually destroy us. Will you be the next one to become seriously wounded or even a casualty? If you are already seriously wounded, will you remain in this state until ultimate failure and disaster? Or if you are wounded, will you use these experiences to eventually make you stronger? If you are not wounded by the enemies of the mind and their comrades, will you keep vigilant to avoid their assaults in the future?

Wounded or not wounded, if you develop a more positive internal dialogue; focus on concrete short as well as long-term goals; maintain an attitude of gratitude; act with constant enthusiasm; be profoundly mindful at all times; plan for a perfect escape; and go deeper by healthy, comprehensive pretending, you can join as a leader in the transcendental army of spiritual warriors. Yes, the enemies of the mind are getting stronger, but the spiritual warrior's ranks are also increasing. As they meet up and join in forces, their love and concern for the rescue of this planet intensifies exponentially. Beloved, join up in order to experience this cosmic, euphoric, blissful, animated association and love. Start by pretending that you are already with us—because you are.

Now, this time when you put the book down, be sure to give it to someone else since it is for them as much as for yourself. Tonight, engage in mindful sleep for there are great adventures ready to support your transformation.

Notes

[1] Gini Graham Scott, Ph.D., *Resolving Conflict with Others and within Yourself.*

[2] Adapted from Phillip C. McGraw, *Life Strategies: Doing What Works, Doing What Matters.*

[3] A. C. Bhaktivedanta Swami Prabhupada, *The Nectar of Instruction.*

[4] All purports from the *Bhagavad-gita* and *Srimad-Bhagavatam* are quoted from A. C. Bhaktivedanta Swami Prabhupada's translations and commentaries on these Vedic scriptures. See full citations in the Bibliography.

[5] Viktor E. Frankl, *Man's Search for Meaning.*

[6] Ian H. Gotlib and Catherine A. Colby. *Treatment of Depression: An Interpersonal Systems Approach.* New York, NY: Pergamon, 1987.

[7] Paul, Robert J. "Managing employee depression in the workplace." Review of Business 24, no. 1 (2003): 31

[8] A.C. Bhaktivedanta Swami Prabhupada, *Krsna: The Supreme Personality of Godhead.*

[9] *Merriam-Webster's Collegiate Dictionary*, s.v. "feng shui."

[10] A.C. Bhaktivedanta Swami Prabhupada, "Conversations, Evening Darsana—August 9, 1976, Tehran," *The Bhaktivedanta VedaBase Ver. 4.11*, CD-ROM, (The Bhaktivedanta Archives, 1998).

[11] Ibid., "Letter to Hamsaduta, June 22, 1972."

[12] Bhayahari Dasa, "Destiny and Endeavor," *Back to Godhead* 36, (January/February 2002): 38

Glossary

Acarya: A spiritual master who teaches by his own example, and who sets the proper religious example for all human beings.

Adhikara: The qualification or ability to understand spiritual matters due to previous spiritual activities.

Ahankara: False ego, by which the soul misidentifies with the material body.

Anartha: Unwanted material desires in the heart that pollute one's consciousness, such as pride, hate, envy, lust, greed, anger, and desires for distinction, adoration, wealth, etc.

Anartha-nivrtti: A stage in the progressive development of devotion to Lord Krishna in which one is freed from unwanted desires and karmic reactions.

Aparadha: An offense.

Arati: A traditional Vedic ceremony during which offerings of incense, ghee lamp, flower, etc. are offered to the Deity of the Lord.

Asrama: The four spiritual orders according to the Vedic social system: *brahmacarya* (student life), *grhastha* (householder life), *vanaprastha* (retirement), and *sannyasa* (renunciation).

Atma: The self (refers sometimes to the body, sometimes to the soul, and sometimes to the senses).

Avadhuta: One who is above all rules and regulations.

Avatara: Literally means "one who descends." A partially or fully empowered incarnation of the Lord who descends from the spiritual sky to the material universe with a particular mission described in the scriptures.

Bhajana: Intimate devotional service; chanting devotional songs in a small group, usually accompanied by musical instruments; solitary chanting.

Bhakta: A devotee of the Lord; one who performs devotional service (*bhakti*).

Bhakti-lata-bija: The seed of the creeper of devotional service.

Bhakti-yoga: The system of cultivation of *bhakti*, or pure devotional service, which is untinged by sense gratification or philosophical speculation.

Bhakti: Devotional service to the Supreme Lord.

Bhava: The stage of transcendental love experienced after transcendental affection; manifestation of ecstatic symptoms in the body of a devotee.

Bhaya: Fear.

Brahmacari: A celibate student under the care of a spiritual master.

Brahmana: A member of the most intelligent class of men, according to the four Vedic occupational divisions of society.

Caranamrta: Remnants of water and other liquids used for bathing the Deity and then mixed with yogurt and sugar.

Dharma: Religious principles; one's natural occupation.

Drdha-vrata: Firm determination.

Gopis: The cowherd girls of Vraja, who are generally the counterparts of Sri Krishna's *hladini-sakti*, Srimati Radharani.

Guru: Spiritual master.

Guru-aparadha: An offense against the spiritual master.

Jnana: The path of empirical knowledge, culminating in attainment of impersonal liberation (*sayujya-mukti*).

Kama: Lust.

Karma: The law of material cause and effect.

Krodha: Anger.

Ksatriya: The martial-spirited, administrative class of Vedic society who protect society from danger.

Lobha: Greed.

Mada: Madness.

Mantra: A pure sound vibration that delivers the mind from its material inclinations and illusions when repeated over and over. A transcendental sound or Vedic hymn, prayer, or chant.

Matsarya: Envy.

Maya: The external energy of the Supreme Lord, which covers the conditioned soul and does not allow him to understand the Supreme Personality of Godhead.

Moha: Bewilderment or illusion.

Mukti: Liberation of a conditioned soul from material consciousness and bondage.

Nistha: Unflinching faith, steadfast devotion; the stage after *anartha-nivrtti*.

Nitya-siddha: An eternally liberated associate of the Lord.

Paramahamsa: A topmost, God-realized devotee of the Supreme Lord.

Paramatma: The Supersoul, the localized aspect of the

Supreme Lord residing in the heart of each embodied living entity and pervading all of material nature.

Parampara: The disciplic succession system of spiritual knowledge beginning with the Lord Himself, and continuing down to the present day.

Prabhu: Master

Prasadam: Spiritual foodstuff.

Pratistha: Fame.

Prayascitta: Atonement for sinful acts.

Prema: Love; pure and unbreakable love of God.

Puja: Worship, usually in the form of making offerings to the Deity of the Lord.

Ruci: Liking, taste.

Sac-cid-ananda-vigraha: The Lord's transcendental form, which is eternal and full of knowledge and bliss.

Sadacara: Good habits or etiquette.

Sadhana: Systematic practices aimed at spiritual perfection, especially Deity worship and chanting the holy name of the Lord.

Sadhana-bhakti: There are nine limbs to the practice of *sadhana-bhakti*: hearing, chanting, remembering, serving, Deity worship, offering everything, friendship, and surrendering everything.

Sadhu: A saintly person.

Sadhu-sanga: The association of *sadhus*.

Sahajiya: A class of so-called devotees who, considering God cheap, ignore the scriptural injunctions and try to imitate the Lord's pastimes.

Sakti: Spiritual energy.

Saktiman: The energetic source, the Supreme Personality of Godhead.

Saktyavesa-avatara: An empowered living entity who serves

as an incarnation of the Lord; empowered by the Supreme Lord with one or more of the Lord's opulences.

Samadhi: Total absorption and trance of the mind and senses in consciousness of the Supreme Godhead and service to Him.

Sambhoga: The ecstasy of the meeting and embracing of lovers.

Samsara: The cycle of repeated birth and death in the material world.

Sanatana-dharma: Literally, the "eternal activity of the soul", or the eternal religion of the living being—to render service to the Supreme Lord, which in this age is executed mainly by chanting the *maha-mantra*.

Saranagati: Surrender.

Sastra: Revealed scripture; Vedic literature.

Sattva-guna: The mode of material goodness.

Siddhanta: Conclusion.

Siddhis: Mystic perfections usually acquired by *yoga* practice and natural to residents of Siddhaloka.

Sisya: Disciple.

Sloka: A Sanskrit verse.

Sraddha: Firm faith and confidence.

Suddha-bhakta: A pure devotee of the Lord.

Sukrti: Result accrued from pious activity.

Svarupa-laksana: The principal symptom (i.e. surrender to Lord Krishna) of a *sadhu* regardless of *varna* and *asrama*.

Utsaha: Enthusiasm.

Vaisnava: A devotee of the Supreme Lord.

Vaisya: A member of the mercantile and agricultural class, according to the four Vedic occupational divisions of society.

Varna: One of the four Vedic social-occupational divisions of society, distinguished by quality of work and situation with regard to the modes of nature.

Vipralamba: Ecstasy in separation.

Vrata: Vow.

Yajna: Sacrifice.

Yoga: Spiritual discipline to link oneself with the Supreme.

Yogi: A transcendentalist who practices one of the many authorized forms of *yoga*, or processes of spiritual purification.

Yuga-dharma: The religion for the age.

Bibliography

Carnegie, Dale. *How to Stop Worrying and Start Living*. New York: Pocket Books, 1984.

Carter, Les and Minirth, Frank M.D. *The Choosing to Forgive Workbook*. Nashville: Thomas Nelson Publishers, 1997.

DeFoore, Bill. *Anger: Deal With It, Heal With It, Stop It From Killing You*. Deerfield Beach, Florida: Health Communications, Inc., 1991.

Frankl, Viktor E. *Man's Search for Meaning*. 4th ed. Translated by Ilse Lasch. Boston: Beacon Press, 1992.

McGraw, Phillip C. *Life Strategies: Doing What Works, Doing What Matters*. New York: Hyperion Books, 1999.

McKay, Matthew; Rogers, Peter D.; and McKay, Judith R.N. *When Anger Hurts: Quieting the Storm Within*. Oakland, CA: New Harbinger Publications, Inc., 1989.

Prabhupada, A. C. Bhaktivedanta Swami. *Bhagavad-gita As It Is*. Los Angeles: Bhaktivedanta Book Trust, 1983.

———. *The Bhaktivedanta VedaBase Ver. 4.11*. CD-ROM. The Bhaktivedanta Archives, 1998.

———. *Krsna: The Supreme Personality of Godhead*. Los Angeles: The Bhaktivedanta Book Trust, 1984.

———. *The Nectar of Devotion*. Los Angeles: Bhaktivedanta Book Trust, 1982.

———. *The Nectar of Instruction*. New York: Bhaktivedanta Book Trust, 1975.

———. *Srimad-Bhagavatam*. 18 vols. Los Angeles: Bhaktivedanta Book Trust, 1987.

———. *Sri Caitanya-caritamrta*. 9 vols. Los Angeles: Bhaktivedanta Book Trust, 1996.

Safer, Jeanne. *Forgiving and Not Forgiving: A New Approach to Resolving Intimate Betrayal*. New York: Avon Books, 1999.

Scott, Gini Graham, Ph.D. *Resolving Conflict with Others and within Yourself*. Oakland, CA: New Harbinger Publications, Inc., 1990.

Thakura, Srila Vrndavana dasa. *Sri Caitanya-bhagavata.* Translated by Kusakratha dasa. N.p., 1993.

Thakura, Visvanatha Cakravarti. *The Bhakti Trilogy: Delineations on the Esoterics of Pure Devotion.* Translated by Sarvabhavana Dasa. Edited by Krsna-rupa Devi Dasi. Calcutta, India: Harmonist Publications, n.d.

Index

Abandoning the association of nondevotees, 126
Acaryas, 37, 41, 43, 101, 102, 118, 125, 126, 129, 148, 197, 199, 202
Accessing our authentic self, 19
Adhikara, 51, 63, 245
Ahankara, 209
Amish, 212, 213
Ananda, 222, 258
Anartha, 255
Anartha-nivrtti, 128, 148, 257
Anarthas, 12, 121, 129, 132, 142, 147, 148, 205
Angas, 248
Anxiety versus excitement, 190
Aparadha, 255
Aparadhas, 41, 123, 147
Apathy
   dangers of, 118

Aprarabdha, 229
Arati, 86, 137
Arcanam, 24, 35, 47, 120
Asa-bandha, 130
Asakti, 128
Asrama, 57, 63, 259
Atma, 24, 47, 120, 170
Atma-nivedam, 24, 47, 120
Attitude
   is crucial, 87
Atyahara, 121
Avadhuta, 256
Avadhuta brahmana, 147
Avatara, 256
Avyartha-kalatvam, 129
Being enthusiastic, 125
Being patient, 125
Bhagavatam, 59

Bhajana, 86, 105, 128
Bhajana-kriya, 128
Bhakta, 94, 259
Bhakti-lata-bija, 256
Bhakti-rasamrta-sindhu, 41
Bhakti-yoga, 35, 36, 96, 236
Bhava, 25, 46, 119, 128, 129, 130, 134, 151, 158, 204, 207
Bhavagad-gita, 193
Bhaya, 12, 112
Bhoga-tyaga, 116, 123, 124
Bhrama, 42
Bhukti, 94
Bijam, 157, 229
Blessed by the Best, 89
Brahmanas, 69, 117, 132, 141
Brhan-naradiya Purana, 35
Caitanya-bhagavata, 93
Caitanya-caritamrta, 64
Capala-sukha, 114, 194
Caranamrta, 87
Change
    initiating, 20
Darsana, 23, 86, 196, 220
Dasyam, 24, 47, 120
Daya-bhak, 95
Desire 232
Devotional service
    six activities spoil, 121
Dhamas, Holy, 199
Dharma, 51, 52, 117, 150, 156, 259, 260
Dhruva, 251
Draupadi, 50
Drdha-vrata, 120, 197

Duhsasana, 132
Durga, 238
Effort versus mercy, 228
Endeavoring with confidence, 125
Enthusiasm
    leads to success, 112
    misdirected, 113
    six principles guarantee, 124
    small achievements increase, 60
    what hinders, 122
Enthusiastic ecstasy, 134
Escape
    consciousness creates, 200
    follow a genuine plan, 195
    on the verge of, 203
Evaluate the goal 53
Excessive false ego, 78
Extraterrestrials, 108
Faithlessness, 119, 144
Fears, 28, 40, 116, 160, 202
Find a project, 55
Find the source, 33
Forgiveness
    importance of, 84
Gandhi, 1
Ghana-tarala, 123
God
    opulences of, 152
Gopis, 134, 137
Gratitude
    access in your own lives, 97
    what supports, 80
Grhasthas, 256
Guidance
    need for, 201
Gunas, 192
Guru, 66

Index   269

Guru-aparadha, 91
Gurukulis, 212
Harinama cintamani, 244
Healthy gratitude, 110
Hladini-sakti, 257
Householders, 39, 40, 143, 215, 256
India, 8, 28, 106
Internal associations
  changing, 31
Introspection, 67, 191
  find time for, 115
Jagannatha, 106, 133
Jnana, 88, 140
Jnana-misra-bhakti, 88, 140
Kali, 24, 35, 39, 147, 208, 239
Kama, 12, 58, 112, 158
Karanapatava, 42
Karma, 4, 5, 18, 19, 32, 37, 64, 88, 90, 124, 140, 217, 227, 228, 229, 230, 231, 233, 234, 236, 241, 242, 245, 250, 251, 252
  influence of, 18
Karma-kanda, 236
Karma-misra-bhakti, 88, 140
Kholaveca, Sridhara, 95
Kirtana, 86, 94
Kirtanam, 24, 47, 120, 125
Kirtanas, 93
Klesa, 229
Krodha, 12, 112
Ksanti, 129
Ksatriyas, 49, 257
Kuta, 229
Laulya, 120, 245
Laziness, 116, 191, 198, 215, 216
Lilas, 131

Limitations
  beyond, 133
Lobha, 12, 112
Mada, 12, 112
Madhurya-Kadambini, 122, 205, 229
Madhya, 64
Mahabharata, 49
Maha-mantra, 259
Mahaprabhu, Caitanya, 94, 95
Mana, 25, 46, 70, 112, 135, 151, 244
Mana-seva, 70, 135, 244
Mana-sunyata, 130
Mantras, 26, 69, 89, 93, 154, 155, 238
Materialistic Activities
  limitations of, 233
Matsarya, 12, 112
Matsya Purana, 229
Miracles through mindfulness, 175
Moha, 12, 112
Mukti, 94
Nama-hatta, 182
Nectar of Instruction, 124, 127
Nistha, 128
Nitya-siddhas, 46, 257
Niyamaksama, 124
Obstacles, 23
Pada-sevanam, 24, 47, 120
Paramahamsa, 61
Paramatma, 91
Parampara, 147
Perfect offering, 132
Permanent solution to the misery, 194

Prabhu, 258
Practice makes perfect, 49
Pramada, 42
Prarabdha, 229, 231
Prasadam, 23, 87
Pratistha, 124
Prayasa, 215
Prayascitta, 236
Prema, 119, 129, 132, 137, 140, 141, 148
Pretend, 20, 221
Pretending
  is the authentic activity, 235
Puja, 31, 95, 183
Recognizing the meaning in life, 81
Remove yourself from the center, 83
Resolute determination, 63
Ruci, 61, 68, 114, 128
Rules and Regulations
  necessary but secondary, 57
Sac-cid-ananda-vigraha, 170, 222, 225, 244
Sadacara, 210
Sadhana, 30, 40, 46, 47, 61, 120, 141, 206, 215, 245, 258
Sadhana-bhakti, 46, 47, 61, 120, 141, 245, 258
Sadhus, 19, 37, 41, 85, 92, 98, 99, 103, 125, 128, 145, 146, 147, 163, 206, 258, 259
Sadhu-sanga, 19, 128
Sahajiyas, 245, 258
Sakhyam, 24, 47, 120
Saktiman, 88, 157
Saktis, 53, 157

Saktyavesa-avataras, 83, 117
Samadhi, 150, 163
Sambhoga, 132
Samsara, 243
Samutkantha, 130
Sanatana-dharma, 52
Sannyasa, 256
Saranagati, 62
Sastra, 92, 98, 125, 145, 146, 147
Sattva-guna, 193
Sayujya-mukti, 257
Scriptures
  hearing from, 93
  pastimes from, 131
Siddhanta, 65, 248
Siddhis, 88, 94
Siksastaka, 71
Sincerity
  is essential, 238
Sisya, 259
Sloka, 71
Smaranam, 24, 47, 120, 125
Soka, 112
Spiritual Life
  essence of, 117
Spiritual Warrior I, 9
Spiritual Warrior II, 9, 80
Spiritual Warrior III, 9
Spiritual Warrior IV, 1, 9, 11, 12, 15, 151
Spiritual Warrior V, 11, 12, 15
Sraddha, 62, 64, 128, 148
Sravanam, 24, 35, 47, 120, 125
Sri Caitanya-caritamrta, 95
Sri Siksastaka, 71

Srimad-Bhagavatam, 17, 47, 58, 68, 75, 95, 96, 111, 137, 147, 187, 203, 224, 251, 261
Stagnation
  causes of, 120
Subjugation, 214
Success
  symptoms of, 128
Suddha-bhaktas, 116, 132
Sukrti, 194
Svarupa, 145, 244, 248
Svarupa-laksana, 145, 248
Taranga-rangini, 124
Thankfulness
  lack of, 78
The Beggar II, 159
The Nectar of Devotion, 95
The Nectar of Instruction, 59, 121, 261
Unhealthy pretending, 222, 226, 227, 243, 244
Utsaha, 62, 114, 123, 124, 128
Utsaha-mayi, 122
Vaisnava-aparadha, 91
Vaisnavas, 134, 146, 199, 244
Vaisya, 141
Vanaprastha, 256
Vandanam, 24, 35, 47, 120
Varnas, 57, 63, 243, 259
Varnasrama-dharma, 57, 58, 63
Vidhi-nisedha, 117
Vinasyati, 59, 121
Vipralambha, 131, 260
Vipralipsa, 42
Virakti, 130
Visada, 112

Visaya-sangara, 123
Vrata, 93, 257
Vyavasayatmika, 64
Vyudha-vikalpa, 123
Yajnas, 97, 260
Yoga, 88, 133, 140, 256, 259, 260
Yoga-misra-bhakti, 88, 140
Yogi, 260
Yuga-dharma, 35, 101

About the Author

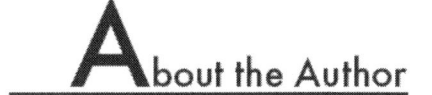

Bhakti-Tirtha Swami Krishnapada was born John E. Favors in a pious, God-fearing family. As a child evangelist he appeared regularly on television. As a young man he was a leader in Dr. Martin Luther King, Jr.'s civil rights movement. At Princeton University he became president of the student council and also served as chairman of the Third World Coalition. Although his main degree is in psychology, he has received accolades in many other fields, including politics, African studies, and international law.

Bhakti-Tirtha Swami's books are used as reference texts in universities and leadership organizations throughout the world. Many of his books have been printed in English, German, French, Spanish, Portuguese, Macedonian, Croatian, Russian, Hebrew, Slovenian, Balinese and Italian.

His Holiness has served as Assistant Coordinator for penal reform programs in the State of New Jersey, Office of the Public

Defender, and as a director of several drug abuse clinics in the United States. In addition, he has been a special consultant for Educational Testing Services in the U.S.A. and has managed campaigns for politicians. Bhakti-Tirtha Swami gained international recognition as a representative of the Bhaktivedanta Book Trust, particularly for his outstanding work with scholars in the former communist countries of Eastern Europe.

Bhakti-Tirtha Swami directly oversees projects in the United States (particularly Washington D.C., Potomac, Maryland, Detroit, Pennsylvania, West Virginia), West Africa, South Africa, Switzerland, France, Croatia and Bosnia. He also serves as the director of the American Federation of Vaisnava Colleges and Schools.

In the United States, Bhakti-Tirtha Swami is the founder and director of the Institute for Applied Spiritual Technology, director of the International Committee for Urban Spiritual Development and one of the international coordinators of the Seventh Pan African Congress. Reflecting his wide range of interests, he is also a member of the Institute for Noetic Sciences, the Center for Defense Information, the United Nations Association for America, the National Peace Institute Foundation, the World Future Society and the Global Forum of Spiritual and Parliamentary Leaders.

A specialist in international relations and conflict resolution, Bhakti-Tirtha Swami constantly travels around the world and has become a spiritual consultant to many high-ranking members of the United Nations, to various celebrities and to several chiefs, kings and high court justices. In 1990 His Holiness was coronated as a high chief in Warri, Nigeria in recognition of his outstanding work in Africa and the world. In recent years, he has met several times with then-President Nelson Mandela of South Africa to share visions and strategies for world peace.

About the Author

In addition to encouraging self-sufficiency through the development of schools, clinics, farm projects and cottage industries, Bhakti-Tirtha Swami conducts seminars and workshops on principle centered leadership, spiritual development, interpersonal relationships, stress and time management and other pertinent topics. He is also widely acknowledged as a viable participant in the resolution of global conflict.

Printed in Great Britain
by Amazon